All of Me for All of Him

A 12-Week Bible Study on Living Fully Surrendered to the Lord

Dr. Lende Click

A surrendered heart is not empty—it is held by God.

Dedication

This Bible study is dedicated to every woman who longs to give God her whole heart.

To the woman who has carried burdens too heavy for her own strength, may you find rest in the faithful hands of the Lord.

To the woman who has wrestled with fear, uncertainty, disappointment, or delay, may you learn that surrender is not the end of hope—it is the beginning of deeper trust.

And to every daughter of the King who desires to live fully yielded to Jesus Christ, may this study remind you that when you give Him all of you, He holds every part of your life with love, mercy, and purpose.

A Note from the Author

Dear sister in Christ,

There are seasons in life when the Lord gently calls us to lay everything before Him—our plans, our worries, our dreams, our pain, our questions, our future, and even the places of our heart we have tried to protect.

Surrender is not always easy. Sometimes it feels like letting go of what we thought life should be. Sometimes it means trusting God when we cannot see the next step. Sometimes it means praying through tears, "Lord, not my will, but Thine be done."

But surrender is not weakness. Surrender is worship.

It is the sacred place where our will bows before God's will. It is the place where fear meets faith, where striving becomes resting, and where the heart learns to trust the One who has never failed.

This Bible study was written to help you walk with the Lord for twelve weeks as you learn to give Him every part of your life. Each week will invite you into Scripture, prayer, reflection, and personal application. You will be encouraged to examine your heart honestly, listen for the Lord's leading, and trust Him more deeply.

My prayer is that through these pages, you will discover the peace of being fully surrendered to Jesus Christ.

A surrendered heart is not empty—it is held by God.

With love in Christ,
Dr. Lende Click

How to Use This Bible Study

This 12-week Bible study is designed for personal devotion, women's Bible study groups, church groups, ministry settings, or quiet time with the Lord.

Each week includes:

- A weekly theme
- Key Scripture
- Opening devotional teaching
- Five daily lessons
- Reflection questions
- Prayer prompts
- Space for journaling and notes
- A weekly surrender prayer

You may complete one lesson each day for five days and use the remaining days for prayer, review, group discussion, or rest. Move slowly and prayerfully. Do not rush the work God is doing in your heart.

Before each lesson, take a moment to pray:

Lord, open my heart to Your Word. Teach me to surrender every part of my life to You. Help me trust You more deeply. In Jesus' name, Amen.

Table of Contents

Introduction: The Beauty of a Surrendered Life

Surrender is one of the most beautiful and difficult lessons in the Christian life.

The world often teaches us to hold tightly to control, protect our plans, depend on our own strength, and make life happen according to our own desires. But the Word of God calls us to a different way. The Lord invites us to lay everything before Him and trust that His hands are wiser, stronger, and more loving than our own.

To surrender to God means to yield our whole life to Him. It means we stop fighting for our own way and begin trusting His way. It means we bring every part of ourselves before the Lord—our heart, mind, will, past, future, relationships, dreams, fears, and calling—and say, "Lord, all that I am belongs to You."

Surrender does not mean we stop caring. It means we care enough to place everything in the hands of the One who knows the end from the beginning.

Surrender does not mean we become passive. It means we become obedient.

Surrender does not mean we have no desires. It means we allow God to purify our desires and align them with His will.

Surrender does not mean life will always be easy. It means we will not walk through life alone.

Jesus showed us the perfect picture of surrender in the garden of Gethsemane. Facing the cross, He prayed, "Father, if thou be willing, remove this cup from me: nevertheless not my will, but thine, be done" (Luke 22:42). His surrender was not without sorrow, but it was full of obedience, trust, and love.

Every believer must come to this same sacred place—not always in the same way, but with the same heart. We must learn to say, "Lord, not my will, but Yours. Not my way, but Yours. Not my timing, but Yours. Not my glory, but Yours."

This Bible study is an invitation to that holy journey.

For the next twelve weeks, you will be encouraged to bring your whole life before the Lord. Some lessons may comfort you. Some may challenge you. Some may bring healing. Some may bring conviction. But through it all, remember this truth:

God never asks you to surrender anything into empty hands. He asks you to surrender into His hands.

And His hands are faithful.

Week 1: The Call to Surrender

Giving Yourself Fully to the Lord

Key Scripture:
"I beseech you therefore, brethren, by the mercies of God, that ye present your bodies a living sacrifice, holy, acceptable unto God, which is your reasonable service."
—Romans 12:1

Weekly Focus

This week is about understanding the call to surrender. Before we can surrender our heart, mind, will, past, future, and plans, we must first understand that surrender begins with offering ourselves fully to God.

Surrender is not giving God the leftover pieces of our lives. It is presenting our whole self to Him as an act of worship.

Opening Devotion

Romans 12:1 gives us a powerful picture of surrender. The apostle Paul urges believers to present their bodies as a living sacrifice unto God. In the Old Testament, sacrifices were placed on the altar before the Lord. But in Christ, we are called to be living sacrifices—not dead offerings, but living, breathing, daily surrendered people who belong fully to God.

This means our surrender is not only a one-time prayer. It is a daily decision.

Every morning, we have the opportunity to say, "Lord, this day belongs to You."

Every difficult moment, we have the opportunity to say, "Lord, I trust You with this."

Every decision, we have the opportunity to say, "Lord, lead me in Your will."

A surrendered life begins when we stop seeing God as someone we simply ask for help, and we begin honoring Him as Lord over everything.

Many believers want God's blessing, protection, healing, and provision, but surrender asks a deeper question: Are we willing to give God authority over all of us?

Surrender says:

Lord, You can have my heart.
Lord, You can have my plans.
Lord, You can have my dreams.
Lord, You can have my pain.
Lord, You can have my future.
Lord, You can have my whole life.

The call to surrender is not a call to lose ourselves. It is a call to find our lives hidden safely in Christ.

Jesus said, "For whosoever will save his life shall lose it: but whosoever will lose his life for my sake, the same shall save it" (Luke 9:24). In God's kingdom, surrender leads to life. Letting go leads to freedom. Yielding leads to peace.

This week, ask the Lord to show you what surrender truly means. Do not be afraid of what He may ask you to release. Anything God asks you to place in His hands is safer there than it could ever be in your own.

Day 1: Surrender Begins with Trust

Read: Proverbs 3:5–6 "Trust in the LORD with all thine heart; and lean not unto thine own understanding. In all thy ways acknowledge him, and he shall direct thy paths."

Surrender begins with trust. We cannot fully surrender to someone we do not trust. This is why the enemy often attacks our view of God. If he can make us doubt God's goodness, faithfulness, or love, then surrender will feel frightening instead of freeing.

But Proverbs 3:5–6 reminds us to trust the Lord with all our heart. Not part of our heart. Not only when life makes sense. Not only when we understand the plan. We are called to trust Him fully.

To surrender means we stop leaning on our own limited understanding and begin leaning on God's perfect wisdom. Our understanding sees only a small part of the story, but God sees the whole picture.

Reflection Questions:

1. What does surrender mean to you personally?

2. Is there an area of your life where you have been leaning on your own understanding instead of trusting God?

3. What truth about God helps you trust Him more deeply?

Prayer:
Lord, help me trust You with all my heart. Forgive me for the times I have leaned on my own understanding more than Your wisdom. Teach me to acknowledge You in all my ways and trust You to direct my path. In Jesus' name, Amen.

Day 2: Presenting Yourself to God

Read: Romans 12:1 "Surrender is not only about giving God our problems. It is about giving God ourselves."

Paul says to present your body as a living sacrifice. This includes your hands, your words, your thoughts, your time, your energy, your service, your decisions, and your daily life. God does not only want Sunday worship. He wants a surrendered life Monday through Saturday too.

When we present ourselves to God, we are saying, "Lord, use me for Your glory."

This kind of surrender changes how we live. It changes what we say yes to. It changes what we say no to. It changes how we treat people. It changes how we spend our time. It changes the desires of our heart.

Reflection Questions:

1. What part of your daily life do you need to present more fully to the Lord?

2. How can your body, words, and actions become worship to God this week?

3. What would it look like for you to live as a "living sacrifice" today?

Prayer:
Lord, I present myself to You. My life belongs to You. Use my hands, my words, my heart, and my steps for Your glory. Help me live as a living sacrifice that is pleasing to You. In Jesus' name, Amen.

Day 3: Surrender Is Worship

Read: Matthew 22:37 "Jesus said unto him, Thou shalt love the Lord thy God with all thy heart, and with all thy soul, and with all thy mind."

Surrender is worship because it gives God the place He deserves. When we surrender, we are declaring that God is Lord, not only with our mouths, but with our lives.

True worship is more than a song. It is a yielded heart. It is obedience. It is trust. It is love that bows before the Lord and says, "You are worthy of all of me."

God does not want divided devotion. He desires our whole heart.

This does not mean we will be perfect. It means we are willing. It means when the Lord reveals something in us that needs to change, we do not harden our hearts. We respond with humility and obedience.

Reflection Questions:

1. In what ways can surrender become worship in your daily life?

2. Are there any areas where your devotion feels divided?

3. What does it mean to love God with all your heart, soul, and mind?

Prayer:
Lord, I want my surrender to be worship before You. Teach me to love You with all my heart, soul, and mind. Remove divided devotion from my life and draw me closer to You. In Jesus' name, Amen.

Day 4: Letting Go of Control

Read: Psalm 37:5 "Commit thy way unto the LORD; trust also in him; and he shall bring it to pass."

One of the hardest parts of surrender is letting go of control. Many times, we hold tightly because we are afraid. We want to know how things will work out. We want to protect ourselves from disappointment. We want to make sure life follows the path we imagined.

But surrender invites us to commit our way unto the Lord.

To commit means to roll the burden onto Him, to entrust the matter into His care. It does not mean we stop praying, working, or obeying. It means we stop carrying what only God can carry.

Control can feel safe, but it often produces anxiety. Surrender may feel uncertain, but it leads to peace because the burden is placed in God's hands.

Reflection Questions:

1. What are you trying to control that God is asking you to surrender?

2. How has trying to control everything affected your peace?

3. What would it look like to commit your way to the Lord today?

Prayer:
Lord, I confess that I often try to control what I should surrender. Help me commit my way to You. Teach me to trust You with the outcome and rest in Your faithful care. In Jesus' name, Amen.

Day 5: Saying Yes to God

Read: Isaiah 6:8 "Also I heard the voice of the Lord, saying, Whom shall I send, and who will go for us? Then said I, Here am I; send me."

A surrendered heart is willing to say yes to God.

Isaiah responded to the call of the Lord with a willing heart: "Here am I; send me." He did not have every detail. He did not know everything the journey would require. But he was available.

Sometimes surrender begins with a simple prayer: "Lord, I am available."

God is not looking for perfect people. He is looking for yielded people. He can use a surrendered heart, a willing spirit, and obedient steps.

Saying yes to God may mean serving in a new way, forgiving someone, releasing a burden, obeying a command, waiting patiently, speaking truth, or walking by faith when you cannot see the full path.

Whatever God asks, remember this: His will is always better than our resistance.

Reflection Questions:

1. What is one area where God may be asking you to say yes?

2. What fear or hesitation makes obedience difficult for you?

3. How can you make yourself available to God this week?

Prayer:
Lord, here I am. I surrender myself to You. Help me say yes to Your will, Your way, and Your timing. Make my heart willing and obedient. Use my life for Your glory. In Jesus' name, Amen.

Week 1 Group Discussion Questions

1. What stood out to you most from this week's study?

2. Why do you think surrender can feel difficult?

3. How does trusting God's character help us surrender more fully?

4. What is one practical step you can take this week to live more surrendered?

Week 1 Surrender Prayer

Lord, I hear Your call to surrender. I do not want to give You only part of my life while holding tightly to the rest. I want to belong fully to You. Teach me to trust You with all my heart. Help me present myself as a living sacrifice, holy and acceptable unto You. Take my plans, my fears, my desires, my questions, and my whole life. I surrender all that I am into Your faithful hands. In Jesus' name, Amen.

Notes

Week 2: Surrendering the Heart

Trusting God with Your Desires, Emotions, and Affections

Key Scripture:
"Keep thy heart with all diligence; for out of it are the issues of life."
—Proverbs 4:23

Weekly Focus

This week is about surrendering the heart to the Lord. The heart is the place of our desires, emotions, affections, longings, disappointments, motives, and loves. When the heart is surrendered to God, the whole life begins to follow Him more faithfully.

God does not only want outward obedience. He wants the heart.

Opening Devotion

The heart is precious to God.

Proverbs 4:23 says, "Keep thy heart with all diligence; for out of it are the issues of life." This means the condition of the heart affects the direction of the life. What fills the heart will often shape the words we speak, the choices we make, the people we follow, the things we desire, and the way we respond to God.

This is why surrendering the heart is so important.

Many times, we surrender our actions before we surrender our affections. We may serve, give, pray, and attend church, but still hold tightly to secret fears, wounds, disappointments, desires, or emotions deep within the heart. The Lord sees those hidden places, and He lovingly invites us to bring them to Him.

Surrendering the heart does not mean pretending we do not feel. It does not mean hiding our emotions or acting strong when we are hurting. It means we allow God into the deepest places of who we are.

We bring Him the joy and the sorrow.
We bring Him the hope and the disappointment.
We bring Him the love and the loneliness.
We bring Him the desires and the fears.
We bring Him the places we understand and the places we cannot explain.

A surrendered heart says, "Lord, search me. Heal me. Lead me. Purify what is not pleasing to You. Hold what is too heavy for me. Teach me to love what You love and release what You ask me to surrender."

The Lord is not careless with the heart that is given to Him. He is gentle, faithful, and true. He does not break the surrendered heart; He restores it. He does not shame the honest heart; He cleanses it. He does not ignore the wounded heart; He heals it with love.

This week, you are invited to open your heart before God. Not just the polished parts. Not just the strong parts. Not just the parts others see. Bring Him all of it.

Because a surrendered heart is not empty—it is held by God.

Day 1: The Heart Belongs to God

Read: Matthew 22:37 "Jesus said unto him, Thou shalt love the Lord thy God with all thy heart, and with all thy soul, and with all thy mind."

Jesus said the greatest commandment is to love the Lord with all the heart, all the soul, and all the mind. This shows us that God desires more than outward religion. He desires love that flows from the inner life.

The heart belongs to God because He created it, knows it, searches it, and loves it. No one understands your heart like the Lord. People may see your actions, hear your words, or notice your emotions, but God sees beneath the surface. He knows the hidden battles, quiet tears, unspoken prayers, and deep desires you may not know how to explain.

Surrendering the heart begins with acknowledging that your heart was made for God. It was not made to be ruled by fear, bitterness, pride, rejection, comparison, or the approval of people. It was made to be filled with the love and truth of the Lord.

When the heart belongs fully to God, we begin to desire what pleases Him. Our love becomes purified. Our motives become examined. Our emotions become submitted to His truth. Our affections become centered on Christ.

This does not happen all at once. It is a daily offering.

Every day, we can pray, "Lord, my heart belongs to You. Search it. Cleanse it. Heal it. Lead it."

Reflection Questions:

1. What does it mean to love the Lord with all your heart?

2. Are there any parts of your heart that feel difficult to surrender to God?

3. What has been ruling your heart lately—faith, fear, peace, worry, love, hurt, or something else?

____

____

Prayer:
Lord, my heart belongs to You. Teach me to love You with all my heart, soul, and mind. Search the hidden places within me and gently lead me into deeper surrender. Help my heart be ruled by Your truth, Your love, and Your peace. In Jesus' name, Amen.

Day 2: Surrendering Hidden Desires

Read: Psalm 37:4 "Delight thyself also in the LORD; and he shall give thee the desires of thine heart."

Desires are not always wrong. God created the heart with the ability to long, hope, dream, love, and desire. But our desires must be surrendered to Him, because an unsurrendered desire can begin to rule us.

Sometimes we desire good things: family, healing, ministry, friendship, provision, purpose, or a door to open. But even good desires must be placed in God's hands. If we hold them too tightly, they can become a source of anxiety, disappointment, jealousy, striving, or impatience.

Psalm 37:4 teaches us to delight in the Lord. Before the desires of the heart are fulfilled, the heart must first be centered in Him. When we delight in the Lord, He shapes our desires. He purifies what needs to be purified. He strengthens what is from Him. He removes what would harm us. He teaches us to want His will above our own way.

Surrendering hidden desires means we are honest with God.

We can say, "Lord, this is what I want, but I trust You with it. If it is from You, prepare me for it. If it is not from You, remove it from my heart. If it is not the right time, help me wait with faith."

God can be trusted with your desires. You do not have to bury them, deny them, or pretend they are not there. Bring them to the Lord and let Him hold them with wisdom.

Reflection Questions:

1. What desire have you been carrying in your heart?

2. Have you surrendered that desire fully to God, or are you still holding tightly to the outcome?

3. How can delighting in the Lord change the way you view your desires?

____

____

Prayer:
Lord, I bring the desires of my heart before You. I do not want anything to rule me except You. Purify my desires, align them with Your will, and help me trust Your timing. If something is not from You, give me grace to release it. If something is from You, prepare me to receive it in Your way. In Jesus' name, Amen.

Day 3: Giving God Emotional Burdens

Read: Psalm 62:8 "Trust in him at all times; ye people, pour out your heart before him: God is a refuge for us. Selah."

God invites His people to pour out their hearts before Him. This is a tender and powerful truth. The Lord does not ask us to hide our emotions from Him. He invites us to bring them honestly into His presence.

Many women carry emotional burdens quietly. They carry grief, pressure, disappointment, rejection, loneliness, worry, exhaustion, or the pain of being misunderstood. Sometimes they keep going on the outside while breaking down on the inside.

But God sees.

Surrendering the heart means giving God the emotions we do not know what to do with. It means pouring them out before Him instead of allowing them to control us. Emotions are real, but they are not meant to be our master. God is our refuge.

When we pour out our hearts to the Lord, we are not informing Him of something He does not know. We are inviting His comfort, truth, and presence into what we are carrying.

You can tell God when you are hurting.
You can tell God when you are afraid.
You can tell God when you feel weary.
You can tell God when you do not understand.
You can tell God when your heart feels heavy.

The surrendered heart does not say, "I must handle this alone." It says, "Lord, this is too heavy for me, but it is not too heavy for You."

Reflection Questions:

1. What emotional burden do you need to pour out before the Lord?

2. Have you been allowing your emotions to lead you, or have you been bringing them to God?

____

____

3. What does it mean to you that God is your refuge?

____

____

Prayer:
Lord, I pour out my heart before You. You see every burden I carry, every tear I have cried, and every emotion I do not know how to explain. Be my refuge. Help me surrender my emotions to Your truth and rest in Your faithful care. In Jesus' name, Amen.

Day 4: Guarding the Heart with Wisdom

Read: Proverbs 4:23 "Keep thy heart with all diligence; for out of it are the issues of life."

To surrender the heart to God does not mean we leave it unguarded. Proverbs tells us to keep, or guard, the heart with all diligence. A surrendered heart must also be a guarded heart.

There are things that can pull the heart away from God: bitterness, envy, pride, offense, ungodly influences, unhealthy relationships, constant comparison, fear, and unhealed wounds. If we are not careful, these things can quietly shape our thoughts, attitudes, and choices.

Guarding the heart does not mean building walls of hardness. It means allowing God's wisdom to protect what He is healing.

A guarded heart is not a cold heart.
A guarded heart is not an unforgiving heart.
A guarded heart is not a fearful heart.

A guarded heart is a heart submitted to God's truth.

Sometimes guarding your heart means being careful what you listen to. Sometimes it means stepping away from conversations that feed bitterness. Sometimes it means setting healthy boundaries. Sometimes it means refusing to rehearse old pain over and over. Sometimes it means choosing prayer instead of panic.

God wants your heart tender toward Him and wise toward what could harm you.

Ask the Lord to show you what has been entering your heart. Ask Him what needs to be removed, healed, forgiven, or surrendered. He is faithful to guide you.

Reflection Questions:

1. What has been influencing your heart the most lately?

2. Is there anything you need to remove, limit, or surrender so your heart can stay close to God?

____

____

3. What healthy boundary may God be leading you to establish with wisdom and grace?

____

____

Prayer:
Lord, help me guard my heart with wisdom. Keep my heart tender toward You and protected from what would pull me away from Your will. Show me what needs to be removed, healed, or surrendered. Let my heart be filled with Your truth and peace. In Jesus' name, Amen.

Day 5: Loving God Above All

Read: Psalm 73:25–26 "Whom have I in heaven but thee? and there is none upon earth that I desire beside thee. My flesh and my heart faileth: but God is the strength of my heart, and my portion for ever."

The deepest surrender of the heart is loving God above all.

This does not mean we stop loving people, enjoying blessings, or caring about the desires God has placed within us. It means God becomes first. He becomes our greatest treasure, our highest love, our strength, and our portion.

The psalmist says, "My flesh and my heart faileth: but God is the strength of my heart." What a beautiful reminder. Our human hearts can grow weak. We can become tired, discouraged, disappointed, or overwhelmed. But God remains the strength of the surrendered heart.

When God is our portion, we are not empty even when life changes. We are not forgotten even when people leave. We are not hopeless even when answers are delayed. We are not destroyed even when our hearts feel weak.

God Himself is enough.

This is not always easy to say, especially in painful seasons. But as we surrender our hearts to the Lord, He teaches us the beauty of desiring Him above everything else. He becomes more precious than what we are waiting for. He becomes more secure than what we are afraid to lose. He becomes more satisfying than what the world can offer.

A heart that loves God above all is a heart that can say, "Lord, even if I do not understand everything, I still choose You."

Reflection Questions:

1. What does it mean for God to be the strength of your heart?

2. Is there anything you have desired more than closeness with God?

3. How can you love God above all in this season of your life?

Prayer:
Lord, be the strength of my heart and my portion forever. Teach me to love You above all things. When my heart feels weak, remind me that You are faithful. When my desires pull me in many directions, bring me back to You. Let my heart belong fully to You. In Jesus' name, Amen.

Week 2 Group Discussion Questions

1. What stood out to you most from this week's study?

2. Why do you think God cares so deeply about the condition of the heart?

3. What is the difference between hiding emotions and surrendering emotions to God?

4. How can we guard our hearts without becoming hard or closed off?

5. What is one desire, burden, or affection you need to place more fully in God's hands?

Week 2 Surrender Prayer

Lord, I surrender my heart to You. I give You my desires, emotions, affections, disappointments, longings, and hidden places. Search my heart and know me. Cleanse what is not pleasing to You. Heal what has been wounded. Guard what You are restoring. Teach me to love You above all and to trust You with every part of my inner life. My heart belongs to You, Lord. Hold it, lead it, and make it fully Yours. In Jesus' name, Amen.

Notes

Week 3: Surrendering the Mind

Letting God Renew Your Thoughts

Key Scripture:
"And be not conformed to this world: but be ye transformed by the renewing of your mind…"
—Romans 12:2

Weekly Focus

This week is about surrendering the mind to the Lord. Our thoughts have great influence over our emotions, choices, words, attitudes, and spiritual walk. A surrendered mind is not ruled by fear, confusion, lies, or the pressure of the world. A surrendered mind is renewed by the truth of God's Word.

Opening Devotion

The mind is a battlefield, but it can also become a place of worship.

Romans 12:2 teaches us not to be conformed to this world, but to be transformed by the renewing of our mind. This means God does not only want to change our outward behavior. He wants to renew the way we think.

Many battles begin in the mind before they ever show up in our actions. A thought can become a fear. A fear can become a belief. A belief can become a decision. A decision can become a direction. This is why surrendering the mind is so important.

The enemy often works through lies, accusations, confusion, worry, comparison, shame, and fear. He may whisper, "You are not enough. God has forgotten you. Nothing will change. You cannot be healed. You are too far behind. You are alone." But the Word of God speaks a greater truth.

God says you are loved.
God says you are not forsaken.
God says He will never leave you.
God says He is your strength.

God says His grace is sufficient.
God says He is able to do exceeding abundantly above all that we ask or think.

Surrendering the mind means we stop letting every thought have authority over us. Not every thought is truth. Not every fear is from God. Not every memory should rule the present. Not every imagination should be followed.

A surrendered mind learns to ask, "Does this thought agree with the Word of God?"

When our minds are renewed, our lives begin to be transformed. We begin to think with faith instead of fear. We begin to respond with wisdom instead of panic. We begin to see ourselves through God's truth instead of old wounds. We begin to walk in peace because our minds are stayed on Him.

This week, invite the Lord into your thought life. Ask Him to reveal the thoughts that need to be surrendered, the lies that need to be replaced, and the truth that needs to be planted deeply within you.

A surrendered mind is a mind held by truth.

Day 1: The Battle of the Mind

Read: 2 Corinthians 10:4–5 "For the weapons of our warfare are not carnal, but mighty through God to the pulling down of strong holds; casting down imaginations, and every high thing that exalteth itself against the knowledge of God…"

The Bible teaches us that there is a spiritual battle, and many times that battle touches the mind. Thoughts, imaginations, and beliefs can rise up against the knowledge of God. When this happens, we must not surrender to the lie. We must surrender the lie to God.

A stronghold can be a pattern of thinking that has become deeply rooted. It may sound like fear, rejection, shame, bitterness, defeat, pride, or unbelief. Sometimes these thoughts have been with us so long that they feel normal. But God's Word has power to pull down what the enemy has built.

The surrendered mind does not ignore the battle. It brings the battle to the Lord.

You do not have to fight mental battles in your own strength. God has given spiritual weapons: prayer, Scripture, worship, truth, faith, and the power of the Holy Spirit. What has felt too strong for you is not too strong for God.

When a thought rises against the truth of God, you can pause and pray: "Lord, I surrender this thought to You. Show me what is true."

The battle of the mind is not won by pretending thoughts are not there. It is won by bringing every thought under the authority of Christ.

Reflection Questions:

1. What thoughts have been battling for your attention lately?

2. Are those thoughts leading you closer to God's truth or farther from His peace?

3. What Scripture truth can you speak over your mind today?

____

____

Prayer:
Lord, I surrender the battle in my mind to You. Pull down every thought, fear, imagination, and belief that rises against Your truth. Teach me to recognize the enemy's lies and stand firmly on Your Word. Renew my mind and fill me with Your peace. In Jesus' name, Amen.

Day 2: Taking Thoughts Captive

Read: 2 Corinthians 10:5 "…and bringing into captivity every thought to the obedience of Christ."

Taking thoughts captive means we do not allow every thought to roam freely in our minds. We bring our thoughts under the lordship of Jesus Christ. We examine them in the light of God's Word.

A thought may come, but it does not have to stay. A fear may speak, but it does not have to lead. A lie may rise, but it does not have to rule.

Many people feel guilty because wrong thoughts come to their minds. But the presence of a thought does not mean you must agree with it. The important question is: What will you do with that thought?

Will you feed it or surrender it?
Will you believe it or test it?
Will you rehearse it or replace it with truth?

Taking thoughts captive is a spiritual discipline. It requires awareness, prayer, and the Word of God. Sometimes we must stop and ask, "Is this thought producing faith or fear? Is this thought rooted in truth or in worry? Is this thought honoring Christ or pulling me away from Him?"

The Lord does not condemn you for needing renewal. He lovingly teaches you how to think according to truth.

A surrendered mind is not a perfect mind. It is a yielded mind.

Reflection Questions:

1. What is one thought you need to take captive today?

2. What would it look like to bring that thought into obedience to Christ?

3. What truth from God's Word can replace that thought?

Prayer:
Lord, help me take every thought captive to the obedience of Christ. Give me wisdom to recognize thoughts that do not come from You. Help me surrender fear, worry, shame, and confusion, and fill my mind with truth. In Jesus' name, Amen.

Day 3: Replacing Lies with Truth

Read: John 8:32

"And ye shall know the truth, and the truth shall make you free."

Freedom comes through truth.

Many of the thoughts that trouble us are rooted in lies. Some lies come from painful experiences. Some come from words spoken over us. Some come from disappointment, rejection, comparison, or spiritual attack. Over time, a lie can begin to feel like truth if it is repeated often enough in the mind.

But Jesus said the truth shall make you free.

A surrendered mind allows God to expose lies and replace them with His Word. This is not always instant. Sometimes the Lord gently reveals one lie at a time and teaches us to stand on one truth at a time.

Lie: I am alone.
Truth: The Lord will never leave me nor forsake me.

Lie: I am not enough.
Truth: God's grace is sufficient for me.

Lie: Nothing good can come from this.
Truth: God is able to work all things together for good to them that love Him.

Lie: My past defines me.
Truth: If any man be in Christ, he is a new creature.

The mind cannot be renewed by emptying it alone. It must be filled with truth. God's Word becomes the light that exposes the lie and the sword that cuts it down.

This is why Scripture must be more than words on a page. It must become truth planted in the heart and mind.

Reflection Questions:

1. What lie have you believed about yourself, your life, or God?

____

____

2. What does God's Word say instead?

____

____

3. How can you begin speaking truth over that area of your life?

____

____

Prayer:
Lord, reveal any lie I have believed and replace it with Your truth. Let Your Word make me free. Help me stop agreeing with fear, shame, and unbelief. Teach me to think according to what You have spoken. In Jesus' name, Amen.

Day 4: Thinking on Things Above

Read: Colossians 3:2 "Set your affection on things above, not on things on the earth."

The mind often follows what it is focused on. When our minds stay fixed on fear, problems, offenses, or earthly pressures, our peace can quickly become disturbed. But Scripture calls us to set our affection on things above.

This does not mean we ignore our responsibilities on earth. It means heaven's truth becomes the lens through which we view our earthly life.

A mind set on things above remembers that God is still sovereign.
A mind set on things above remembers that this world is not our final home.
A mind set on things above remembers that obedience matters.
A mind set on things above remembers that Christ is greater than every burden.

What we repeatedly think about can either strengthen faith or strengthen fear. This is why we must be careful with what we allow to fill our minds. The conversations we entertain, the media we consume, the worries we rehearse, and the memories we revisit can all shape our focus.

Surrendering the mind means asking God to lift our thoughts higher.

Instead of only thinking about the problem, we remember the Provider. Instead of only thinking about the battle, we remember the Victory. Instead of only thinking about what is uncertain, we remember the One who never changes.

Reflection Questions:

1. What has been occupying most of your thoughts lately?

2. How can you set your mind more intentionally on things above?

3. What earthly concern do you need to view through the truth of God's
    kingdom?

Prayer:
Lord, lift my thoughts above fear, worry, and earthly distractions. Help me set my
affection on things above. Teach me to see my life through Your truth and to
remember that You are greater than every burden I face. In Jesus' name, Amen.

Day 5: Peace for a Surrendered Mind

Read: Isaiah 26:3 "Thou wilt keep him in perfect peace, whose mind is stayed on thee: because he trusteth in thee."

God promises perfect peace to the one whose mind is stayed on Him. This does not mean life will be without trouble. It means the mind can be anchored in God even when life feels uncertain.

Peace does not come from controlling every circumstance. Peace comes from trusting the Lord in every circumstance.

A surrendered mind does not have to figure everything out. It rests in the One who knows all things. A surrendered mind does not have to rehearse every fear. It returns again and again to the faithfulness of God. A surrendered mind does not have to be ruled by confusion. It asks the Lord for wisdom and waits on His leading.

There may be days when you must surrender the same thought many times. That does not mean you are failing. It means you are learning to bring your mind back to God. Every time you turn from worry to prayer, you are practicing surrender. Every time you choose truth over fear, you are strengthening faith. Every time you fix your thoughts on the Lord, you are making room for peace.

God is able to keep your mind.

You may not be able to control every thought that comes, but you can choose where your mind will dwell. Let it dwell on the Lord. Let it dwell on His Word. Let it dwell on His faithfulness. Let it dwell on His promises.

A surrendered mind becomes a resting place for God's peace.

Reflection Questions:

1. What does it mean for your mind to be stayed on the Lord?

2. Where do you need God's peace in your thought life?

3. What can you do when worry tries to take over your mind?

Prayer:
Lord, keep my mind in perfect peace as I trust in You. Help my thoughts stay fixed on Your goodness, Your truth, and Your faithfulness. When worry rises, lead me back to prayer. When fear speaks, lead me back to Your Word. Let my mind rest in You. In Jesus' name, Amen.

Week 3 Group Discussion Questions

1. What stood out to you most from this week's study?

2. Why is the mind such an important place of surrender?

3. What are some common lies believers may struggle with, and what truths from Scripture can replace them?

4. How can we take thoughts captive in a practical way during daily life?

5. What helps you keep your mind stayed on the Lord when life feels
    overwhelming?

Week 3 Surrender Prayer

Lord, I surrender my mind to You. Renew my thoughts by the power of Your Word.
Pull down every stronghold, cast down every imagination that rises against Your
truth, and help me bring every thought into obedience to Christ. Replace lies with
truth, confusion with wisdom, fear with faith, and worry with peace. Teach me to set
my mind on things above and keep my thoughts stayed on You. In Jesus' name,
Amen.

Notes

Week 4: Surrendering the Will

Learning to Say, "Not My Will, But Thine Be Done"

Key Scripture:
"Nevertheless not my will, but thine, be done."
—Luke 22:42

Weekly Focus

This week is about surrendering the will to the Lord. Our will is the place of our choices, decisions, preferences, plans, and desires for how life should go. To surrender the will means we learn to trust God's will above our own, even when His way is difficult, unexpected, or different from what we imagined.

Opening Devotion

One of the most sacred prayers ever spoken was prayed by Jesus in the garden of Gethsemane: "Nevertheless not my will, but thine, be done."

This prayer was not spoken from a comfortable place. It was spoken in agony, surrender, obedience, and love. Jesus knew the suffering before Him. He knew the weight of the cross. Yet in the deepest moment of sorrow, He yielded His will to the Father.

This shows us that surrender is not always easy. Sometimes surrender comes with tears. Sometimes it comes with trembling. Sometimes it comes when our hearts are breaking and our flesh wants another way.

But true surrender says, "Lord, I trust Your will more than my understanding."

The human will often wants control. We want our timing, our plan, our answer, our direction, our comfort, our outcome. But the surrendered will bows before God and says, "You are Lord. You know best. Lead me."

Surrendering the will does not mean our desires never matter to God. It means God's wisdom becomes greater than our preference. It means obedience becomes more important than comfort. It means we stop wrestling against the Lord and begin resting in His authority.

There is peace in a yielded will.

A stubborn will can keep us striving, anxious, offended, and exhausted. A surrendered will may still walk through hard places, but it walks with trust. It knows that the Father is faithful, even when His will leads through a valley before it leads to victory.

Jesus surrendered in the garden before He carried the cross. Because of His obedience, salvation was made available to the world. His surrender brought eternal fruit.

In the same way, our surrender may produce fruit we cannot yet see. Our obedience may bless lives beyond our understanding. Our yielded yes to God may open doors of purpose that our own plans never could.

This week, ask the Lord to show you where your will needs to bow. Not because God wants to take something good from you, but because He wants to lead you into what is holy, fruitful, and aligned with His purpose.

A surrendered will says, "Lord, not my way, but Yours."

Day 1: The Example of Jesus

Read: Luke 22:42 "Saying, Father, if thou be willing, remove this cup from me: nevertheless not my will, but thine, be done."

Jesus is our perfect example of surrender. In the garden of Gethsemane, He prayed honestly before the Father. He did not hide the weight of what was before Him. He said, "If thou be willing, remove this cup from me." Yet He also prayed, "Nevertheless not my will, but thine, be done."

This teaches us that surrender is not dishonest. Jesus shows us that we can bring our deepest feelings, fears, and desires to the Father. We can tell Him when something feels heavy. We can ask Him for help. We can pour out our hearts before Him.

But surrender does not stop with honesty. It moves from honesty into yielded trust.

Jesus did not choose the easy path. He chose the Father's will. His obedience was costly, but it was holy. His surrender was painful, but it was powerful. His yielded will became the doorway of redemption.

When we look at Jesus, we learn that surrender is love in action. It is trust that obeys. It is faith that bows. It is devotion that says, "Father, I trust You even here."

The surrendered life begins by following the surrendered Savior.

Reflection Questions:

1. What does Jesus' prayer in the garden teach you about surrender?

2. Is there a place in your life where you need to pray, "Not my will, but Thine be done"?

3. How does Jesus' example give you courage to surrender your own will?

Prayer:
Lord Jesus, thank You for showing me the beauty of a surrendered will. Teach me to pray honestly and trust fully. Help me follow Your example and yield my will to the Father, even when the path is hard. Let my surrender become an act of love and obedience. In Jesus' name, Amen.

Day 2: When God's Will Is Different from Ours

Read: Isaiah 55:8–9 "For my thoughts are not your thoughts, neither are your ways my ways, saith the LORD."

There are times when God's will is different from what we expected. We may pray for one door, but God closes it. We may ask for one answer, but He leads another way. We may imagine a certain timeline, but He asks us to wait. We may think we know what is best, but God sees what we cannot see.

This can be difficult for the heart. When God's will is different from ours, we may feel confused, disappointed, or even afraid. But Isaiah reminds us that God's thoughts are higher than our thoughts and His ways are higher than our ways.

Higher does not always mean easier. Higher means wiser. Higher means holier. Higher means God sees the beginning, the middle, and the end.

Surrendering the will means we stop demanding that God explain everything before we obey Him. It means we trust His character when we do not understand His plan.

Sometimes the Lord protects us through a closed door. Sometimes He redirects us through delay. Sometimes He matures us through waiting. Sometimes He changes our desires because He is preparing something better than what we imagined.

A surrendered will can say, "Lord, this is not what I expected, but I trust You."

God is not cruel when His will differs from ours. He is faithful. He leads His children with wisdom, love, and eternal purpose.

Reflection Questions:

1. Have you ever experienced God leading you in a way that was different from your plan?

2. What makes it difficult to trust God when His will is different from yours?

3. What truth about God helps you surrender when you do not understand?

Prayer:
Lord, Your thoughts are higher than my thoughts and Your ways are higher than my ways. Help me trust You when Your will is different from what I expected. Give me grace to release my plan and follow Yours with faith. In Jesus' name, Amen.

Day 3: Obedience in the Hard Places

Read: 1 Samuel 15:22 "Behold, to obey is better than sacrifice, and to hearken than the fat of rams."

Obedience is one of the clearest signs of a surrendered will.

It is possible to do many religious things and still resist God in one area. We can sing, serve, give, attend church, and speak spiritual words, yet still hold back obedience when God touches something we do not want to surrender.

But Scripture says, "To obey is better than sacrifice." God is not only looking for outward offerings. He is looking for a yielded heart that obeys His voice.

Obedience in the hard places may mean forgiving when the flesh wants to hold offense. It may mean speaking truth when silence feels safer. It may mean waiting when we want to rush. It may mean letting go when we want to hold on. It may mean serving faithfully when no one sees. It may mean saying no to something that pulls us away from God.

Hard obedience is still holy obedience.

God does not ask for obedience to harm us. He asks for obedience because His way leads to life. Disobedience may feel easier in the moment, but it often produces heaviness, distance, and regret. Obedience may feel costly, but it produces peace, growth, and intimacy with God.

A surrendered will does not only obey when it is convenient. It obeys because God is worthy.

Reflection Questions:

1. Is there an area where God has been asking for your obedience?

2. What makes obedience difficult in that area?

3. What step of obedience can you take this week?

Prayer:
Lord, give me a heart that obeys You. Show me any area where I have resisted Your will. Help me choose obedience even when it is hard, uncomfortable, or costly. I want my life to please You more than I want my own way. In Jesus' name, Amen.

Day 4: The Blessing of a Yielded Will

Read: Psalm 40:8 "I delight to do thy will, O my God: yea, thy law is within my heart."

There is a beautiful change that happens when the will becomes yielded to God. At first, surrender may feel like a struggle. But over time, as we grow in trust, we begin to delight in God's will.

Psalm 40:8 says, "I delight to do thy will, O my God." This is more than duty. This is love. This is the heart learning that God's will is not a burden meant to crush us, but a path meant to lead us closer to Him.

The blessing of a yielded will is peace. We no longer have to fight against God's leading. We no longer have to carry the pressure of controlling every outcome. We no longer have to live divided between what we want and what God is asking.

A yielded will brings rest because it says, "Lord, You lead. I will follow."

This does not mean every step becomes easy. It means we are no longer walking in resistance. Resistance makes the soul weary. Surrender brings the soul into agreement with God.

When God's will becomes our desire, obedience becomes worship. We begin to see His commands as protection, His correction as love, His timing as wisdom, and His direction as mercy.

There is blessing in yielding—not always the blessing of getting what we wanted, but the deeper blessing of becoming more like Christ.

Reflection Questions:

1. What blessing have you experienced when you yielded to God's will?

2. Where do you need peace that comes from surrender instead of control?

3. How can obedience become worship in your life?

Prayer:
Lord, teach me to delight in Your will. Change my heart so obedience becomes worship and surrender becomes peace. Help me stop resisting what You are asking of me. Let Your will become precious to me. In Jesus' name, Amen.

Day 5: Choosing God's Way

Read: Proverbs 3:6 "In all thy ways acknowledge him, and he shall direct thy paths."

Surrendering the will becomes practical in daily choices. It is not only about the big decisions of life. It is also about the small moments when we choose whether to follow our flesh or follow the Lord.

Will I respond with anger or with grace?
Will I walk in fear or in faith?
Will I seek revenge or choose forgiveness?
Will I rush ahead or wait on God?
Will I follow my own understanding or acknowledge Him in all my ways?

Proverbs 3:6 gives a beautiful promise: when we acknowledge the Lord in all our ways, He shall direct our paths. This means God is not only concerned with church decisions or ministry decisions. He wants to be acknowledged in every part of life.

A surrendered will asks God, "Lord, what pleases You here?"

This question can change everything. It invites God into our choices, our relationships, our words, our spending, our serving, our resting, our planning, and our responding.

Choosing God's way may not always be popular. It may not always be understood by others. It may require humility, patience, courage, and faith. But God's way is always the right way.

Every time you choose God's way, you strengthen the habit of surrender. Every yes to Him makes the next yes more natural. Every act of obedience teaches your heart that the Lord can be trusted.

A surrendered life is built one yielded choice at a time.

Reflection Questions:

1. In what daily choices do you need to acknowledge the Lord more intentionally?

2. What does choosing God's way look like in your current season?

3. How can small acts of obedience shape a surrendered life?

Prayer:
Lord, help me acknowledge You in all my ways. Direct my path and teach me to choose Your way in both big and small decisions. Give me courage to obey, humility to follow, and faith to trust Your direction. In Jesus' name, Amen.

Week 4 Group Discussion Questions

1. What stood out to you most from this week's study?

2. Why can it be difficult to pray, "Not my will, but Thine be done"?

3. How does Jesus' example in the garden help us understand surrender?

4. What is the difference between outward religious activity and true obedience?

5. What is one area where God may be asking you to choose His way over your own?

____

____

____

Week 4 Surrender Prayer

Lord, I surrender my will to You. Teach me to pray with a faithful heart, "Not my will, but Thine be done." Forgive me for the times I have resisted Your direction or trusted my own way more than Yours. Help me obey You in the hard places and delight in Your will. Lead my choices, guide my steps, and make my heart willing to follow You wherever You lead. In Jesus' name, Amen.

Notes

____

____

____

____

____

____

____

____

____

____

Week 5: Surrendering the Past

Giving God Your Pain, Regrets, and Wounds

Key Scripture:
"Remember ye not the former things, neither consider the things of old. Behold, I will do a new thing…"
—Isaiah 43:18–19

Weekly Focus

This week is about surrendering the past to the Lord. The past may hold memories, wounds, regrets, shame, disappointments, losses, and painful seasons that still touch the heart today. But God is able to heal, redeem, restore, and bring new life where there has been brokenness.

Opening Devotion

The past can be a heavy place to carry.

Some memories bring joy and gratitude. Others bring tears, regret, shame, grief, or questions that have never been fully answered. Many women keep walking forward on the outside while still carrying pain from yesterday on the inside.

But God does not ask His daughters to carry the past alone.

Isaiah 43:18–19 says, "Remember ye not the former things, neither consider the things of old. Behold, I will do a new thing…" This does not mean the past did not matter. It does not mean we pretend nothing happened. It means the past does not have the final word when God is still working.

Surrendering the past means placing every memory, wound, regret, and disappointment into the hands of the Lord. It means allowing Him to touch the places we may have hidden, avoided, or tried to fix in our own strength.

Some parts of the past may need healing.
Some parts may need forgiveness.
Some parts may need release.

Some parts may need truth spoken over them.
Some parts may need to be grieved before they can be surrendered.

God is gentle with wounded hearts. He does not rush the healing work. He does not shame the tears. He does not despise the broken places. Psalm 147:3 says, "He healeth the broken in heart, and bindeth up their wounds."

The enemy may try to use the past as a prison. He may remind you of what happened, what you did, what was done to you, what you lost, or what you wish you could change. But Jesus came to set the captives free. He does not only forgive sin. He restores souls. He does not only see the wound. He brings healing to the wound.

A surrendered past says, "Lord, I cannot change what happened, but I trust You to heal me, teach me, redeem me, and lead me forward."

This week, you are invited to bring your past before God—not to relive it in fear, but to release it in faith. The Lord is able to bring beauty from ashes, purpose from pain, and testimony from tears.

Your past may be part of your story, but it is not greater than God's power to redeem.

Day 1: God Sees What You Survived

Read: Psalm 56:8 "Thou tellest my wanderings: put thou my tears into thy bottle: are they not in thy book?"

God sees what you survived.

There are things people may never fully understand. There may be tears you cried in secret, battles you fought quietly, seasons you endured with little support, and wounds that were never seen by others. But none of it was hidden from God.

Psalm 56:8 gives a tender picture of the Lord's care. He knows our wanderings and gathers our tears. This shows us that God is not distant from our pain. He is near. He remembers what others forgot. He sees what others missed. He values what others dismissed.

Surrendering the past begins with knowing that God saw it. You do not have to prove your pain to Him. You do not have to explain every detail for Him to care. He already knows.

Sometimes healing begins when the heart whispers, "Lord, You saw me."

The past may have made you feel invisible, but you were never invisible to God. The pain may have made you feel abandoned, but you were never outside His sight. The journey may have felt lonely, but the Lord was present, even in the places you could not feel Him.

God's seeing is not passive. He sees with compassion. He sees with justice. He sees with love. He sees with power to restore.

Bring Him the part of your past that still feels unseen. Let the Lord remind you that every tear matters to Him.

Reflection Questions:

1.   What part of your past do you need to remember God saw and cared about?

2. Have you ever felt unseen or misunderstood in your pain?

3. How does it comfort you to know that God keeps record of your tears?

Prayer:
Lord, thank You for seeing what I survived. Thank You for knowing every tear, every hurt, and every hidden battle. Help me believe that I was never forgotten by You. Bring comfort to the places of my heart that have felt unseen. In Jesus' name, Amen.

Day 2: Releasing Regret and Shame

Read: Romans 8:1 "There is therefore now no condemnation to them which are in Christ Jesus…"

Regret looks back and says, "I wish I had done differently." Shame goes deeper and says, "Something is wrong with me." Both can become heavy burdens if they are not surrendered to the Lord.

There are moments in life we may wish we could change. Words we wish we had not spoken. Choices we wish we had not made. Seasons we wish we had handled differently. But living chained to regret does not heal the past. It only keeps the heart trapped in what cannot be undone.

Romans 8:1 declares that there is now no condemnation to them which are in Christ Jesus. This is a powerful truth for the surrendered heart. Conviction from God leads us to repentance, healing, and restoration. Condemnation from the enemy keeps us trapped in shame, hopelessness, and self-punishment.

There is a difference between godly sorrow and shame. Godly sorrow turns the heart toward God. Shame tries to make the heart hide from Him.

Surrendering regret and shame means we bring our failures, mistakes, and painful memories to Jesus. We confess what needs confession. We receive forgiveness where forgiveness has been given. We accept grace where shame has tried to rule.

Jesus did not die on the cross so His people could live forever under condemnation. He came to forgive, cleanse, redeem, and make new.

You cannot go back and rewrite yesterday, but God can redeem what is surrendered to Him today.

Reflection Questions:

1. Is there a regret from your past that still weighs on your heart?

2. How can you tell the difference between conviction from God and
    condemnation from the enemy?

____

____

3. What truth from Romans 8:1 do you need to receive personally?

____

____

Prayer:
Lord, I surrender regret and shame to You. Forgive me for the places where I have
sinned, and heal me from the places where shame has tried to define me. Help me
receive Your mercy and walk in the freedom You have given through Christ Jesus. In
Jesus' name, Amen.

Day 3: Letting God Heal the Wounds

Read: Psalm 147:3 "He healeth the broken in heart, and bindeth up their wounds."

God is a healer of broken hearts.

Some wounds are easy to recognize. Others are hidden beneath years of strength, survival, busyness, or silence. A person can smile and still be wounded. A person can serve and still be hurting. A person can love God deeply and still need healing in places that were broken long ago.

Psalm 147:3 tells us that the Lord heals the broken in heart and binds up their wounds. This means God does not ignore emotional pain. He tends to it. He comes near to the broken places with compassion and care.

Healing often requires surrender because we must allow God into the places we may have tried to protect. Sometimes we protect our wounds by avoiding them. Sometimes we protect them by becoming hard. Sometimes we protect them by pretending we are fine. But the Lord cannot heal what we refuse to bring into His light.

Letting God heal the wounds does not mean the pain was small. It means God is greater.

Healing may come through prayer, Scripture, wise counsel, forgiveness, grief, community, and time. The Lord may work gently and gradually. He may uncover layers. He may lead you to release what you have carried for years. Trust His process.

God is not impatient with healing. He is faithful in it.

The wound that is surrendered to God can become a place where His mercy is revealed. The scar may remain as part of your story, but it no longer has to bleed with the same pain. God can touch what was broken and make it a testimony of His grace.

Reflection Questions:

1. Is there a wound from the past that still needs God's healing touch?

2. Have you been protecting that wound instead of bringing it to the Lord?

____

____

3. What step might God be inviting you to take toward healing?

____

____

Prayer:
Lord, heal the broken places in my heart. I surrender the wounds I have carried, hidden, or tried to protect. Bind up what has been painful and restore what has been damaged. I trust You to heal me with mercy, truth, and love. In Jesus' name, Amen.

Day 4: Forgiveness and Freedom

Read: Ephesians 4:32 "And be ye kind one to another, tenderhearted, forgiving one another, even as God for Christ's sake hath forgiven you."

Forgiveness is one of the hardest and most freeing acts of surrender.

When someone has hurt us, betrayed us, rejected us, or wounded us deeply, forgiveness can feel impossible in our own strength. The pain may feel too real. The injustice may feel too heavy. The memory may still feel fresh, even years later.

But forgiveness is not saying the wrong was acceptable. It is not pretending the pain did not happen. It is not always restoring trust or removing needed boundaries. Forgiveness means releasing the debt into God's hands and refusing to let bitterness rule the heart.

Unforgiveness keeps the past alive in the present. It allows the wound to continue speaking. It can quietly shape our emotions, relationships, thoughts, and spiritual life. But God calls us to forgive because He desires freedom for His children.

Ephesians 4:32 reminds us that we forgive because God, for Christ's sake, has forgiven us. We do not forgive because the pain was small. We forgive because the mercy of God is great.

Sometimes forgiveness is a decision before it becomes a feeling. Sometimes we must pray, "Lord, I am willing to be made willing." Sometimes forgiveness happens in layers as God heals the heart.

Forgiveness does not mean you must give unsafe people access to your life. Wisdom and forgiveness can walk together. Boundaries can be holy. But bitterness must be surrendered.

A surrendered past releases the right to revenge and trusts God to be righteous, just, and faithful.

Reflection Questions:

1. Is there someone you need God's help to forgive?

2. What has unforgiveness cost your heart, peace, or spiritual life?

3. How can forgiveness and healthy boundaries both be part of wisdom?

Prayer:
Lord, help me forgive as You have forgiven me. I surrender bitterness, resentment, and the desire for revenge. Heal the pain that made forgiveness feel impossible. Give me wisdom for healthy boundaries and grace to walk in freedom. In Jesus' name, Amen.

Day 5: Trusting God to Do a New Thing

Read: Isaiah 43:19 "Behold, I will do a new thing; now it shall spring forth; shall ye not know it?"

God is able to do a new thing.

The past may explain part of your story, but it does not have the power to cancel God's purpose. What happened to you, what you lost, what you regret, or what you survived is not greater than the redeeming power of the Lord.

Isaiah 43:19 is a promise of hope. God says, "Behold, I will do a new thing." The word behold invites us to look again. It is as if God is saying, "Do not only stare at what was. Look at what I am able to do."

Sometimes the heart becomes so used to looking backward that it struggles to recognize the new work God is beginning. Pain can make us expect more pain. Disappointment can make us afraid to hope. Regret can make us believe we are disqualified. But God is not finished.

Surrendering the past opens the heart to God's new work.

The new thing may begin quietly. It may begin as peace where there was anxiety. It may begin as courage where there was fear. It may begin as forgiveness where there was bitterness. It may begin as trust where there was control. It may begin as a small step forward when you thought you were stuck forever.

Do not despise the beginning of healing. Do not overlook small signs of grace. God often starts new things in hidden places before they are seen openly.

Your past is not too broken for God to redeem. Your heart is not too wounded for God to restore. Your story is not too far gone for God to rewrite with mercy.

Trust Him. He is able to do a new thing.

Reflection Questions:

1. Where do you need to believe God can do a new thing in your life?

2. Have you been looking backward so much that it is hard to see what God may be doing now?

3. What small sign of healing, growth, or hope can you thank God for today?

Prayer:
Lord, I believe You are able to do a new thing. Help me stop living chained to the past and teach me to walk forward in faith. Redeem what has been painful, restore what has been broken, and open my eyes to the new work You are doing in me. In Jesus' name, Amen.

Week 5 Group Discussion Questions

1. What stood out to you most from this week's study?

2. Why can it be difficult to surrender the past to God?

3. How does knowing God sees our tears bring comfort and healing?

4. What is the difference between conviction and condemnation?

5. How can forgiveness bring freedom without removing the need for wisdom
    and healthy boundaries?

Week 5 Surrender Prayer

Lord, I surrender my past to You. I give You every wound, regret, shame,
disappointment, loss, and painful memory. Thank You for seeing every tear and
knowing every hidden place of my heart. Heal what has been broken, forgive what
needs forgiveness, and free me from what has held me captive. Help me release
bitterness, receive Your mercy, and trust You to do a new thing in my life. My past is
in Your hands, and You are faithful to redeem. In Jesus' name, Amen.

Notes

Week 6: Surrendering the Future

Trusting God with What You Cannot See

Key Scripture:
"For I know the thoughts that I think toward you, saith the LORD…"
—Jeremiah 29:11

Weekly Focus

This week is about surrendering the future to the Lord. The future can bring questions, hopes, fears, dreams, decisions, and unknown paths. But God already sees what we cannot see, and He is faithful to lead His children one step at a time.

Opening Devotion

The future can feel exciting, frightening, or uncertain.

There may be things you are praying for, waiting for, hoping for, or afraid of. You may wonder what will happen next, how God will provide, where He will lead, or whether the dreams in your heart will ever come to pass. Sometimes the unknown can feel heavier than what is already known.

But God is not uncertain about your future.

Jeremiah 29:11 reminds us that the Lord knows His thoughts toward His people. His plans are not confused, careless, or cruel. He sees the road ahead. He knows the turns, delays, open doors, closed doors, battles, blessings, and lessons that are still before you.

Surrendering the future means placing tomorrow into the hands of the God who is already there.

It means we stop demanding to see the whole map before we obey the next instruction. It means we release the fear of what might happen and trust the One who holds all things together. It means we bring our hopes and concerns before the Lord and say, "Father, I trust You with what I cannot see."

The future belongs to God, not to fear.

Fear tries to fill the unknown with worst-case possibilities. Faith fills the unknown with confidence in God's character. Fear says, "What if everything goes wrong?" Faith says, "Even then, God will be faithful."

Surrendering the future does not mean we never plan. Scripture teaches wisdom, preparation, and stewardship. But our plans must bow before God's will. We can make plans with open hands, trusting that the Lord has the right to direct, delay, change, or establish them according to His purpose.

Proverbs 16:9 says, "A man's heart deviseth his way: but the LORD directeth his steps."

This is a comfort, not a threat. God's direction is mercy. His guidance is protection. His timing is wisdom. His purpose is greater than our limited understanding.

This week, you are invited to surrender what is ahead. Bring God your questions, dreams, fears, decisions, and unknowns. He may not show you every detail, but He will be faithful to lead you.

The future is safest in the hands of the Lord.

Day 1: God Already Knows Tomorrow

Read: Psalm 139:16 "Thine eyes did see my substance, yet being unperfect; and in thy book all my members were written…"

God is not surprised by tomorrow.

Before you ever arrived at this moment, the Lord knew your days. He knew your beginning, your journey, your struggles, your needs, your calling, and every step ahead. Nothing in your future is hidden from His sight.

This truth brings peace to the surrendered heart. You do not have to know everything, because God already does. You do not have to carry tomorrow's burdens today, because the Lord who gives grace for today will also give grace for tomorrow.

Many times, anxiety grows when we try to live in a day God has not yet asked us to carry. We imagine situations that may never happen. We rehearse conversations that may never take place. We worry about provision before the need arrives. We try to solve future problems with today's strength.

But God gives daily grace.

Surrendering the future begins with remembering that God already knows what is ahead. He sees what you cannot see, and He is able to prepare, provide, protect, and guide.

You are not walking into an unknown future alone. You are walking with a known God.

Reflection Questions:

1. What part of the future feels uncertain or heavy to you right now?

2. How does it comfort you to know that God already sees tomorrow?

3. What future burden have you been trying to carry today?

Prayer:
Lord, thank You that tomorrow is not hidden from You. Help me stop carrying future burdens with today's strength. Teach me to trust that You already know what is ahead and that You will give me grace for every step. In Jesus' name, Amen.

Day 2: Faith Beyond What You Can See

Read: 2 Corinthians 5:7 "For we walk by faith, not by sight."

Faith is often required most when we cannot see the next step clearly.

If God showed us every detail of the future, we might not need to trust Him in the same way. But the Christian life is a walk of faith. We follow the Lord not because we can see everything, but because we trust the One who leads us.

Walking by faith does not mean walking blindly. It means walking with confidence in God's character, God's Word, and God's presence. Even when the path is unclear, God Himself is faithful.

There may be seasons when all you have is enough light for the next step. The Lord may not reveal the whole journey at once. He may simply say, "Trust Me here. Obey Me today. Follow this step."

Faith beyond what you can see says, "Lord, I do not know how everything will work out, but I know You are good."

It says, "I do not have all the answers, but I have Your promise."

It says, "I cannot see the end, but I can trust Your hand."

The surrendered future is not built on perfect understanding. It is built on faith in a perfect God.

Reflection Questions:

1. Where is God asking you to walk by faith and not by sight?

2. What makes it hard for you to trust when you cannot see the full picture?

3. What promise from God's Word can strengthen your faith today?

Prayer:
Lord, help me walk by faith and not by sight. When I cannot see the full path, remind me that I can trust Your hand. Strengthen my faith, quiet my fears, and teach me to follow You one step at a time. In Jesus' name, Amen.

Day 3: Surrendering the Need to Know

Read: Deuteronomy 29:29 "The secret things belong unto the LORD our God: but those things which are revealed belong unto us…"

One of the hardest parts of surrendering the future is surrendering the need to know.

Many of us want answers before we obey. We want details before we trust. We want timing before we rest. We want assurance that everything will happen the way we hope. But God does not always give us every answer at once.

Deuteronomy 29:29 reminds us that some things belong to the Lord. There are details He may choose not to reveal yet. There are answers we may not understand in this season. There are reasons that may remain hidden until the right time.

This does not mean God is withholding because He is unkind. It means He is God, and we are His children. He knows what we are ready to carry. He knows what should be revealed now and what should remain in His hands.

Surrendering the need to know means we stop making peace dependent on having all the details. Our peace comes from God's presence, not from complete information.

It is okay to ask God questions. It is okay to seek wisdom. It is okay to pray for direction. But when God has not revealed something, we can still trust Him.

A surrendered heart can say, "Lord, I do not know, but You do."

That simple prayer can bring rest to a weary soul.

Reflection Questions:

1. What answer or detail have you been longing to know?

2. Has your peace been depending on knowing the outcome?

3. How can you trust God with what He has not yet revealed?

Prayer:
Lord, I surrender my need to know every detail. Help me trust You with the secret things that belong to You. Give me wisdom for what You have revealed and peace for what You have not. My future is safe in Your hands. In Jesus' name, Amen.

Day 4: Walking One Step at a Time

Read: Psalm 119:105 "Thy word is a lamp unto my feet, and a light unto my path."

God's Word is a lamp unto our feet and a light unto our path. A lamp does not always show the whole road far ahead. It gives enough light for the next step.

This is often how God leads His people.

We may want the full plan, but God gives the next instruction. We may want the final destination, but God gives light for today. We may want to know how everything will come together, but God asks us to obey the step in front of us.

Walking one step at a time requires humility. It teaches us dependence. It keeps us close to the Lord because we must continue listening, praying, and trusting.

Sometimes the next step is simple obedience. Sometimes it is waiting. Sometimes it is making a wise decision. Sometimes it is having a difficult conversation. Sometimes it is resting instead of striving. Sometimes it is preparing quietly for what God has not yet opened publicly.

Do not despise the next small step.

A surrendered future is not always revealed in one dramatic moment. Often, it unfolds through daily faithfulness. One prayer. One act of obedience. One decision to trust. One step forward. One day at a time.

The Lord knows how to guide you. His Word will not fail you. His presence will not leave you. His timing will not be late.

Follow the light He has given today.

Reflection Questions:

1. What is the next step God may be asking you to take?

2. Have you been waiting for the whole path before obeying the next step?

3. How can God's Word guide your decisions in this season?

Prayer:
Lord, Your Word is a lamp unto my feet and a light unto my path. Help me follow the light You have given today. Give me courage for the next step, patience for the process, and trust for the journey ahead. In Jesus' name, Amen.

Day 5: Hope in God's Faithfulness

Read: Lamentations 3:22–23 "It is of the LORD'S mercies that we are not consumed, because his compassions fail not. They are new every morning: great is thy faithfulness."

The future can be surrendered because God is faithful.

His mercies are new every morning. His compassion does not fail. His faithfulness does not expire. The same God who carried you yesterday will be faithful tomorrow.

When we think about the future, we often focus on what we do not know. But faith invites us to focus on what we do know: God is good. God is faithful. God is present. God is wise. God is able. God keeps His promises.

Hope is not pretending there will never be difficulties. Hope is confidence that God will remain faithful through whatever comes.

You may not know what next month holds. You may not know what next year will bring. You may not know how the prayer will be answered, how the provision will come, how the door will open, or how the situation will change. But you can know this: God will be faithful.

A surrendered future rests in God's proven character.

Look back for a moment. Has the Lord carried you before? Has He made a way before? Has He comforted you before? Has He provided strength when you thought you could not continue? His past faithfulness becomes courage for your future surrender.

The God who has been faithful is the God who will be faithful.

Reflection Questions:

1. Where have you seen God's faithfulness in your past?

2. How can remembering His faithfulness help you surrender your future?

3. What hope do you need to hold onto today?

Prayer:
Lord, great is Your faithfulness. Thank You for new mercies every morning. Help me face the future with hope, not fear. Remind me of all the ways You have carried me before, and teach me to trust that You will be faithful again. In Jesus' name, Amen.

Week 6 Group Discussion Questions

1. What stood out to you most from this week's study?

2. Why can the future feel difficult to surrender?

3. What is the difference between wise planning and trying to control the future?

4. How can we walk by faith when we cannot see the whole path?

5. What reminder of God's faithfulness gives you courage for what is ahead?

Week 6 Surrender Prayer

Lord, I surrender my future to You. I give You my questions, dreams, fears, hopes, decisions, and unknowns. Help me stop carrying tomorrow's burdens with today's strength. Teach me to walk by faith and not by sight. Give me peace when You have not revealed every detail, and guide me one step at a time through Your Word. I trust that You already know what is ahead, and I believe You will be faithful. In Jesus' name, Amen.

Notes

Week 7: Surrendering Fear and Worry

Resting in the Faithfulness of God

Key Scripture:
"Casting all your care upon him; for he careth for you."
—1 Peter 5:7

Weekly Focus

This week is about surrendering fear, worry, anxiety, and burdens to the Lord. Fear can make the heart feel unsafe, and worry can make the mind tired. But God invites His children to cast every care upon Him because He cares for them.

Opening Devotion

Fear and worry can feel heavy on the soul.

Fear often looks at what could happen. Worry keeps turning it over in the mind again and again. Together, they can steal peace, drain strength, and make the heart forget that God is near.

But the Lord gives us a beautiful invitation in 1 Peter 5:7: "Casting all your care upon him; for he careth for you." God does not tell us to carry our cares better. He tells us to cast them upon Him. He does not shame us for having burdens. He invites us to bring them to Him.

This is tender and personal. The verse does not only say God is powerful, though He is. It does not only say God is sovereign, though He is. It says He cares for you.

The God who holds the universe also cares about the burden on your heart.

Surrendering fear and worry means we stop letting them rule us. It does not mean we never feel concern. It means when fear rises, we bring it to the Lord. When worry circles in the mind, we turn it into prayer. When the burden feels too heavy, we place it in God's hands again.

Fear says, "You are alone."
God says, "I will never leave thee, nor forsake thee."

Worry says, "What if there is not enough?"
God says, "My grace is sufficient for thee."

Fear says, "You cannot handle this."
God says, "I am thy strength."

Worry says, "Everything depends on you."
God says, "Cast thy burden upon the LORD, and he shall sustain thee."

The surrendered life is not a life without storms. It is a life anchored in the One who speaks peace in the storm.

This week, you are invited to bring every fear and worry before the Lord. Not just the big burdens. Not just the spiritual-sounding concerns. Bring all of it. The Lord cares for you.

A surrendered heart can rest because it is held by a faithful God.

Day 1: God Cares for You

Read: 1 Peter 5:7 "Casting all your care upon him; for he careth for you."

One of the most healing truths a worried heart can receive is this: God cares for you.

Not just for the world in general. Not just for the church as a whole. Not just for someone else who seems stronger or more spiritual. He cares for you personally.

Every care matters to Him. The burden that keeps you awake at night matters. The concern you have not spoken aloud matters. The fear you feel embarrassed to admit matters. The small worry you think you should be able to handle matters.

God invites you to cast all your care upon Him. All means all. Not only the cares you think are important enough. Not only the cares you cannot solve. Not only the cares that feel urgent. Every care can be brought to Him.

To cast your care upon the Lord means to transfer the weight from your hands to His. It is an act of trust. It says, "Lord, this is too much for me, but it is not too much for You."

Sometimes we give God a burden in prayer, then pick it back up in worry. When that happens, we can return again. Surrender is often practiced repeatedly. Every time we bring the care back to God, we are learning to trust Him more deeply.

You are not a burden to God. Your cares are not too small for Him. Your heart is not too complicated for Him. He cares for you.

Reflection Questions:

1. What care do you need to cast upon the Lord today?

2. Do you truly believe God cares about the details of your life? Why or why not?

3.   What makes it difficult for you to release burdens into God's hands?

____

____

Prayer:
Lord, thank You for caring for me. I cast my cares upon You today—the big ones, the small ones, the hidden ones, and the heavy ones. Teach me to trust Your love and stop carrying what You have invited me to surrender. In Jesus' name, Amen.

Day 2: When Fear Speaks Loudly

Read: Isaiah 41:10 "Fear thou not; for I am with thee: be not dismayed; for I am thy God..."

Fear can speak loudly.

It can speak through thoughts, circumstances, memories, reports, delays, or uncertainty. Fear often tries to sound convincing. It tells us what might go wrong. It reminds us of past pain. It imagines future trouble. It makes the heart feel surrounded before anything has even happened.

But God's voice is greater than fear.

Isaiah 41:10 says, "Fear thou not; for I am with thee." The command not to fear is connected to the promise of God's presence. God does not simply say, "Do not be afraid." He says, "Do not be afraid, because I am with you."

The answer to fear is not our own strength. The answer to fear is God's presence.

When fear speaks loudly, we must learn to let God's truth speak louder. We can answer fear with Scripture. We can answer fear with prayer. We can answer fear by remembering who God is.

Fear says, "What if you are alone?"
Truth says, "God is with me."

Fear says, "What if you are not strong enough?"
Truth says, "God will strengthen me."

Fear says, "What if everything falls apart?"
Truth says, "God will uphold me with the right hand of His righteousness."

Surrendering fear does not always mean feelings disappear instantly. It means fear no longer gets the final word. God does.

Reflection Questions:

1. What fear has been speaking loudly in your life?

2. What truth from Isaiah 41:10 do you need to speak over that fear?

____

____

3. How can you let God's voice become louder than fear this week?

____

____

Prayer:
Lord, when fear speaks loudly, help me hear Your voice more clearly. Remind me that You are with me, You are my God, You will strengthen me, and You will uphold me. I surrender fear to Your faithful presence. In Jesus' name, Amen.

Day 3: The Peace of Prayer

Read: Philippians 4:6–7 "Be careful for nothing; but in every thing by prayer and supplication with thanksgiving let your requests be made known unto God."

Prayer is one of God's gifts for the worried heart.

Philippians 4:6–7 teaches us not to be anxious, but in everything to bring our requests to God by prayer and supplication with thanksgiving. Then the peace of God, which passes all understanding, will keep our hearts and minds through Christ Jesus.

This is a beautiful exchange. We bring God our worry, and He gives peace. We bring requests, and He guards our hearts. We bring burdens, and He meets us with His presence.

Prayer does not always change the situation immediately, but it changes where the burden rests. Instead of carrying worry alone, we place it before the Father. Instead of letting anxiety circle endlessly in our minds, we turn it into conversation with God.

The phrase "with thanksgiving" is important. Thanksgiving reminds the heart of God's faithfulness. It helps us remember what He has already done. It shifts our focus from fear of what may happen to trust in the God who has never failed.

When worry rises, pray.
When fear returns, pray.
When your mind feels restless, pray.
When you do not know what to do, pray.
When you are waiting for an answer, pray with thanksgiving.

The peace of God may not make sense to others. It may even pass your own understanding. But it is real, and it is able to guard your heart and mind through Christ Jesus.

Reflection Questions:

1. What worry do you need to turn into prayer today?

2. How has prayer brought peace to you in past seasons?

____

____

3. What can you thank God for while you wait for His answer?

____

____

Prayer:
Lord, I bring my worries to You in prayer. Thank You for hearing me, caring for me, and guarding my heart with Your peace. Help me turn anxious thoughts into prayer and remember Your faithfulness with thanksgiving. In Jesus' name, Amen.

Day 4: Trusting God in the Storm

Read: Mark 4:39–40 "And he arose, and rebuked the wind, and said unto the sea, Peace, be still…"

The disciples knew what it felt like to be afraid in a storm. The wind was strong, the waves were filling the ship, and fear took hold of their hearts. Yet Jesus was with them in the boat.

That truth matters: Jesus was with them in the storm.

Sometimes we believe that if God is with us, storms should not come. But Scripture shows us that His presence does not always mean the absence of storms. It means we are not alone in them.

Jesus spoke to the wind and the sea, saying, "Peace, be still." The storm had to obey His voice. The same Lord who calmed the sea is able to calm the fear in our hearts.

Trusting God in the storm means remembering who is in the boat with us. It means we do not measure God's care by the size of the waves. It means we trust His authority even when the wind is loud.

Some storms end quickly. Some last longer than we expected. Some change our direction. Some reveal our need for deeper faith. But no storm is greater than Christ.

When fear rises in the storm, cry out to Jesus. He is not far away. He is present, powerful, and faithful.

A surrendered heart can say, "Lord, even here, I trust You."

Reflection Questions:

1. What storm are you facing, or what storm have you recently walked through?

2. How does it encourage you to remember that Jesus is with you in the storm?

3. Where do you need Him to speak, "Peace, be still" in your life?

Prayer:
Lord Jesus, thank You for being with me in every storm. When the wind feels loud and my heart feels afraid, remind me of Your power and presence. Speak peace over my heart and teach me to trust You even here. In Jesus' name, Amen.

Day 5: Resting Instead of Striving

Read: Matthew 11:28–30 "Come unto me, all ye that labour and are heavy laden, and I will give you rest."

Jesus invites the weary to come to Him.

He does not say, "Try harder until you are no longer tired." He does not say, "Carry it alone and prove your strength." He says, "Come unto me…and I will give you rest."

Fear and worry often lead to striving. We try to fix everything, control everything, understand everything, and prevent everything. We carry burdens God never asked us to carry. We exhaust ourselves trying to be strong in our own strength.

But Jesus offers rest.

Rest is not laziness. Rest is trust. It is the soul learning to lean on Christ instead of striving in the flesh. It is doing what God asks while leaving the outcome in His hands. It is obeying without carrying the weight of being God.

There is a holy relief that comes when we realize we are not the Savior. We are not the Provider. We are not the Keeper of all things. God is.

Surrendering fear and worry means choosing rest over striving. It means coming to Jesus with the heavy load and allowing Him to teach us His way. His yoke is easy, and His burden is light.

The Lord is not calling you to collapse under the weight of your cares. He is calling you to come closer.

Bring Him the burden. Receive His rest.

Reflection Questions:

1. Where have you been striving instead of resting in the Lord?

2. What burden do you need to bring to Jesus today?

____

____

3. What would trusting rest look like in your daily life?

____

____

Prayer:
Lord Jesus, I come to You weary and heavy laden. I surrender my striving, fear, and worry. Teach me to rest in You, trust Your care, and walk in Your peace. Thank You that I do not have to carry what belongs in Your hands. In Jesus' name, Amen.

Week 7 Group Discussion Questions

1. What stood out to you most from this week's study?

____

____

2. Why do fear and worry often feel difficult to surrender?

____

____

3. How does knowing God cares for you personally change the way you carry burdens?

____

____

4. What is one practical way to turn worry into prayer?

____

____

5. What does resting in Jesus look like during a busy or difficult season?

Week 7 Surrender Prayer

Lord, I surrender my fear and worry to You. I cast every care upon You because You care for me. When fear speaks loudly, help me hear Your truth more clearly. When worry fills my mind, teach me to pray with thanksgiving. When storms come, remind me that Jesus is with me. Help me stop striving in my own strength and receive the rest You freely give. My heart is safe in Your faithful hands. In Jesus' name, Amen.

Notes

Week 8: Surrendering in the Waiting

Trusting God's Timing

Key Scripture:
"Wait on the LORD: be of good courage, and he shall strengthen thine heart..."
—Psalm 27:14

Weekly Focus

This week is about surrendering to the Lord in seasons of waiting. Waiting can test the heart, stretch faith, and reveal what we are truly trusting. But God's timing is never careless. He is working even when we cannot see the answer yet.

Opening Devotion

Waiting is one of the hardest places to surrender.

It is one thing to trust God when the answer comes quickly. It is another thing to trust Him when days, months, or even years pass and the promise still seems far away. Waiting can make the heart tired. It can bring questions, discouragement, impatience, or fear that God has forgotten.

But God does not waste waiting seasons.

Psalm 27:14 says, "Wait on the LORD: be of good courage, and he shall strengthen thine heart." This verse does not say waiting will always feel easy. It tells us to be of good courage because the Lord will strengthen the heart.

Waiting on God is not the same as doing nothing. It is active trust. It is choosing faith when the answer has not arrived. It is praying when the door has not opened. It is obeying when the timeline is unclear. It is worshiping while the heart still has questions.

The waiting season can become a holy place where God deepens our roots.

In the waiting, He teaches patience.
In the waiting, He purifies motives.

In the waiting, He strengthens faith.
In the waiting, He prepares us for what we are praying for.
In the waiting, He reminds us that He is the treasure, not only the answer.

Sometimes God delays because He is protecting us. Sometimes He waits because He is preparing the right time. Sometimes He is working in people, places, and circumstances we cannot see. Sometimes He is doing a deeper work in us before He changes what is around us.

A surrendered heart learns to say, "Lord, I trust Your timing more than my impatience."

Waiting does not mean God is absent. Silence does not mean He has stopped caring. Delay does not mean denial. The Lord is faithful in the hidden places.

This week, bring your waiting season to God. Bring the unanswered prayers, the delayed dreams, the uncertain doors, and the weary places of your heart. He will strengthen you as you wait.

A surrendered heart can wait because it knows the One it is waiting on.

Day 1: Waiting Is Not Wasted

Read: Isaiah 40:31 "But they that wait upon the LORD shall renew their strength…"

Waiting can feel like nothing is happening, but in God's hands, waiting is never wasted.

Isaiah 40:31 promises that those who wait upon the Lord shall renew their strength. This means God can do something within us while we are waiting for something around us. He can renew strength, deepen trust, shape character, and prepare the heart.

Many times, we only measure progress by visible movement. We think if the answer has not arrived, then nothing is changing. But God often works beneath the surface first. Like roots growing deeper before fruit appears, the waiting season can be a place where faith becomes stronger and the soul becomes more anchored in Him.

Waiting may reveal what we have been leaning on. It may show us where we are impatient, fearful, controlling, or discouraged. But revelation is not condemnation. It is an invitation to surrender more deeply.

God can use the waiting to prepare you for what He is preparing for you.

Do not despise hidden growth. Do not assume delay means failure. Do not believe the lie that your prayers are forgotten. The Lord is still present, still working, and still faithful.

Waiting is not wasted when it is surrendered to God.

Reflection Questions:

1. What are you waiting on God for in this season?

2. How might God be strengthening or preparing you during this waiting season?

3. What would change if you believed your waiting was not wasted?

Prayer:
Lord, help me believe that my waiting is not wasted. Renew my strength while I wait on You. Teach me to trust Your hidden work, even when I cannot see visible progress. Prepare my heart for Your will and Your timing. In Jesus' name, Amen.

Day 2: Strength for the Waiting Season

Read: Psalm 27:14 "Wait on the LORD: be of good courage, and he shall strengthen thine heart…"

Waiting can make the heart feel weak.

When the answer is delayed, courage can feel thin. Hope can feel tired. Faith can feel tested. You may wonder how much longer you can keep praying, believing, serving, or trusting.

But Psalm 27:14 gives a promise: "He shall strengthen thine heart." God does not ask you to create your own strength while you wait. He promises to strengthen you.

This is a beautiful mercy. The Lord knows waiting can be hard. He knows the weight of unanswered questions. He knows the ache of delay. He knows the courage it takes to keep trusting when nothing appears to be changing.

Strength for the waiting season often comes day by day. God may not give strength for the whole journey at once, but He gives grace for today. He strengthens the heart through His Word, His presence, prayer, worship, encouragement, and quiet reminders of His faithfulness.

Sometimes strength looks like peace for one more day.
Sometimes strength looks like the courage to pray again.
Sometimes strength looks like choosing not to give up.
Sometimes strength looks like worshiping with tears.
Sometimes strength looks like resting instead of striving.

You are not weak because waiting feels hard. You are human. And the Lord is faithful to strengthen His children.

Reflection Questions:

1. Where does your heart need strength in this waiting season?

2. How has God strengthened you in past seasons of waiting?

3. What is one way you can receive strength from the Lord this week?

Prayer:
Lord, strengthen my heart while I wait. When I feel tired, renew me. When I feel discouraged, lift me. When I feel weak, remind me that Your strength is greater than mine. Help me be of good courage because You are faithful. In Jesus' name, Amen.

Day 3: When God Seems Silent

Read: Habakkuk 2:3 "For the vision is yet for an appointed time… though it tarry, wait for it; because it will surely come, it will not tarry."

There are seasons when God seems silent.

You may pray and not hear an answer. You may seek direction and still feel unsure. You may wait for a door to open, but nothing changes. Silence can feel confusing, especially when your heart truly desires to obey God.

But silence does not mean absence.

God may be quiet, but He is not inactive. He may not be speaking in the way you expected, but He is still present. He may not reveal the answer yet, but He is still guiding, preparing, and working according to His appointed time.

Habakkuk 2:3 reminds us that the vision is for an appointed time. God's timing is not random. What He appoints, He knows how to fulfill. Though it tarries, we are told to wait for it.

Waiting during silence requires faith that trusts God's character more than emotional clarity. Feelings may say, "God is far away." Faith says, "The Lord is near, even when I cannot feel Him." Feelings may say, "Nothing is happening." Faith says, "God is working in ways I cannot see."

When God seems silent, keep doing what He has already told you to do. Keep praying. Keep obeying. Keep walking in truth. Keep worshiping. Keep your heart tender.

The teacher is often quiet during the test, but the teacher is still present.

Reflection Questions:

1. Have you ever walked through a season when God seemed silent? What was that like?

2. What truth helps you trust God when you do not feel clear answers?

3. What has God already told you to do that you can continue doing faithfully?

Prayer:
Lord, when You seem silent, help me trust that You are still near. Strengthen my faith when I do not have answers. Teach me to keep obeying what You have already shown me and to wait for Your appointed time. In Jesus' name, Amen.

Day 4: Patience as Surrender

Read: James 1:4 "But let patience have her perfect work, that ye may be perfect and entire, wanting nothing."

Patience is a form of surrender.

It says, "Lord, I will not rush ahead of You." It says, "I will not force a door You have not opened." It says, "I will not let impatience lead me into disobedience." It says, "I trust Your timing more than my urgency."

James 1:4 teaches us to let patience have her perfect work. This means patience is doing something in us. It is forming maturity. It is shaping endurance. It is teaching us to remain steady while God works.

Impatience often comes from fear. We fear missing out. We fear being forgotten. We fear it will be too late. We fear someone else is moving ahead while we are still waiting. But surrendered patience rests in the truth that God knows the right time.

Patience does not mean we stop caring. It means we refuse to let urgency become our master.

When patience has her perfect work, the heart becomes less controlled by panic and more anchored in God. We become steadier. We learn to wait without becoming bitter. We learn to hope without demanding. We learn to pray without trying to control the answer.

A surrendered heart can wait patiently because it knows God is never late.

Reflection Questions:

1. Where is God teaching you patience right now?

2. How can impatience lead to striving or disobedience?

3. What would it look like to let patience have her perfect work in you?

Prayer:
Lord, teach me patience as surrender. Help me not to rush ahead, force doors, or let fear control my timing. Let patience have her perfect work in me. Make my heart steady, faithful, and trusting while I wait on You. In Jesus' name, Amen.

Day 5: Courage While You Wait

Read: Psalm 31:24 "Be of good courage, and he shall strengthen your heart, all ye that hope in the LORD."

Waiting requires courage.

It takes courage to keep hoping when the answer has not come. It takes courage to keep praying when the situation looks the same. It takes courage to keep obeying when the promise feels delayed. It takes courage to trust God's timing when your heart longs for movement.

Psalm 31:24 says, "Be of good courage, and he shall strengthen your heart, all ye that hope in the LORD." Courage is not pretending waiting is easy. Courage is choosing to hope in the Lord even when waiting is hard.

Your hope is not in the timeline. Your hope is not in perfect circumstances. Your hope is not in your ability to make things happen. Your hope is in the Lord.

That is why you can be courageous.

While you wait, keep your heart close to God. Do not let delay make you distant. Do not let disappointment make you bitter. Do not let uncertainty make you stop believing. Bring every feeling to the Lord and let Him strengthen you again.

Courage while waiting may look quiet. It may look like getting up and serving faithfully another day. It may look like praying again. It may look like worshiping through tears. It may look like saying, "Lord, I still trust You."

The waiting season will not last forever, but the faithfulness of God will.

Be of good courage. The Lord is strengthening your heart.

Reflection Questions:

1. What does courage look like for you in this waiting season?

2. Where do you need to place your hope back in the Lord instead of in the timeline?

3. What is one faithful step you can take while you wait?

Prayer:
Lord, give me courage while I wait. Strengthen my heart and help me hope in You. Keep me from bitterness, fear, and discouragement. Teach me to remain faithful, prayerful, and surrendered until Your appointed time. In Jesus' name, Amen.

Week 8 Group Discussion Questions

1. What stood out to you most from this week's study?

2. Why can waiting be such a difficult place of surrender?

3. How can waiting become a place of spiritual growth instead of only frustration?

4. What helps you trust God when He seems silent?

5. What is one way you can practice courage and patience while you wait?

Week 8 Surrender Prayer

Lord, I surrender my waiting season to You. I give You the prayers that feel delayed, the answers I still long for, and the timeline I do not understand. Help me believe that waiting is not wasted when it is placed in Your hands. Strengthen my heart, teach me patience, and give me courage to keep hoping in You. I trust Your appointed time, Your hidden work, and Your faithful love. In Jesus' name, Amen.

Notes

Week 9: Surrendering Your Plans and Dreams

Letting God Lead Your Steps

Key Scripture:
"A man's heart deviseth his way: but the LORD directeth his steps."
—Proverbs 16:9

Weekly Focus

This week is about surrendering plans, dreams, goals, expectations, and personal timelines to the Lord. God is not against dreams, but He desires that every dream be placed under His wisdom, timing, and will. A surrendered life makes plans with open hands and trusts God to direct every step.

Opening Devotion

Plans and dreams can be beautiful gifts.

God has created us with the ability to hope, imagine, prepare, build, serve, and desire fruitful things. Dreams can give direction. Plans can help us steward time and opportunities wisely. Goals can encourage faithfulness and discipline.

But even good plans and dreams must be surrendered to the Lord.

Proverbs 16:9 says, "A man's heart deviseth his way: but the LORD directeth his steps." This verse reminds us that planning is not wrong, but our plans are not meant to rule over God's direction. We may make plans, but the Lord has the authority to establish, delay, change, close, open, or redirect our steps.

This can be difficult when we have prayed over a dream, worked hard toward a goal, or imagined life unfolding a certain way. When plans change, the heart can feel disappointed or confused. We may wonder if we heard God wrong, if we failed, or if the dream is over.

But sometimes a changed plan is not a failed plan. Sometimes it is divine redirection.

God sees what we cannot see. He knows what doors are good for us and what doors would harm us. He knows when we are ready and when more preparation is needed. He knows what dreams came from Him, what dreams need refining, and what dreams need to be released.

Surrendering your plans and dreams does not mean you stop dreaming. It means you stop making the dream lord over your life. Christ remains Lord. The dream becomes something you steward, not something you worship.

A surrendered dream says, "Lord, if this is from You, lead it. If this needs to change, shape it. If this is not Your will, help me release it. If this is for a later time, help me wait faithfully."

There is peace in knowing that God's plan is better than our best plan without Him.

This week, you are invited to place every plan and dream before the Lord. Bring Him what you hope for, what you are building, what you are afraid to lose, and what you do not understand. Let Him lead your steps.

A dream surrendered to God is safest in His hands.

Day 1: When Plans Change

Read: Proverbs 19:21 "There are many devices in a man's heart; nevertheless the counsel of the LORD, that shall stand."

Plans can change quickly.

A door may close. A timeline may shift. A relationship may change. A ministry opportunity may not unfold as expected. A dream may take longer than we hoped. Life may move in a direction we did not plan.

When plans change, the heart can feel unsettled. We may feel disappointed, frustrated, embarrassed, or afraid. But Proverbs 19:21 reminds us that while there may be many plans in the heart, the counsel of the Lord shall stand.

This truth brings comfort. Our plans may change, but God's purpose does not fall apart. What surprises us does not surprise Him. What feels like interruption to us may be part of His instruction, protection, or redirection.

Surrendering when plans change means we bring the disappointment honestly to God, but we do not let disappointment become distrust. We may grieve what did not happen, but we keep believing that the Lord is still wise and faithful.

Changed plans do not mean God has abandoned you.

Sometimes He closes a door because He is guarding your future. Sometimes He slows the timeline because He is preparing your heart. Sometimes He redirects your steps because His purpose is larger than what you first imagined.

When plans change, pray before you panic. Ask the Lord, "What are You teaching me here? How do You want me to follow You now?"

The surrendered heart can trust that God is still leading, even when the plan looks different.

Reflection Questions:

1. What plan in your life has changed or taken longer than expected?

2. How do you usually respond when plans do not go the way you hoped?

____

____

3. How can you trust the counsel of the Lord when your own plans change?

____

____

Prayer:
Lord, help me trust You when my plans change. I surrender my disappointment, confusion, and desire for control. Remind me that Your counsel shall stand and Your purpose will not fail. Teach me to follow You with faith, even when the path looks different than I expected. In Jesus' name, Amen.

Day 2: Dreams in God's Hands

Read: Psalm 37:5 "Commit thy way unto the LORD; trust also in him; and he shall bring it to pass."

Dreams become safest when they are committed to the Lord.

Psalm 37:5 teaches us to commit our way unto the Lord and trust Him. To commit something to God means to place it in His care. It means we stop trying to carry the dream in our own strength and allow the Lord to lead, shape, and establish what is pleasing to Him.

Some dreams are deeply personal. They may involve family, ministry, writing, healing, purpose, service, provision, or a new beginning. Because dreams can touch the deepest part of the heart, surrendering them can feel vulnerable.

But God can be trusted with what matters to you.

If a dream is from Him, He knows how to nurture it. If it needs refinement, He knows how to purify it. If it needs to wait, He knows the right season. If it is not His best, He knows how to gently redirect your heart.

A dream in God's hands may not unfold according to your exact timeline, but it will be under His care.

Sometimes we cling to dreams because we fear losing them. But surrender does not destroy what God has ordained. Surrender protects the dream from becoming an idol. It keeps our hearts attached to the Giver more than the gift.

You can work faithfully while still surrendering fully. You can prepare diligently while still trusting God with the outcome. You can dream with hope while keeping your hands open before the Lord.

Reflection Questions:

1. What dream do you need to commit to the Lord more fully?

2. Have you been carrying this dream in your own strength?

____

____

3. What would it look like to trust God with both the dream and the outcome?

____

____

Prayer:
Lord, I commit my dreams to You. I place my hopes, desires, and goals in Your faithful hands. Lead what is from You, refine what needs changing, and help me release anything that is not Your will. I trust You with the dream and the outcome. In Jesus' name, Amen.

Day 3: Letting God Redirect You

Read: Proverbs 3:5–6 "Trust in the LORD with all thine heart; and lean not unto thine own understanding. In all thy ways acknowledge him, and he shall direct thy paths."

Redirection can feel uncomfortable.

Many times, we want God to bless the path we already chose, but surrender allows God to direct the path according to His wisdom. Proverbs 3:5–6 reminds us not to lean on our own understanding, but to acknowledge Him in all our ways.

Letting God redirect you requires humility. It means admitting that your understanding is limited. It means trusting that God may see danger, delay, preparation, or purpose that you cannot see. It means being willing to follow when He leads differently than expected.

Redirection is not rejection.

Sometimes when God redirects us, we feel as if something has been taken away. But often, He is leading us toward something better, deeper, safer, or more fruitful. A closed door may be mercy. A changed plan may be protection. A new direction may be preparation for a greater purpose.

The Lord's direction may come through Scripture, prayer, wise counsel, circumstances, conviction, peace, or a gentle check in the spirit. We must stay close enough to listen and humble enough to obey.

A surrendered heart can say, "Lord, I wanted that way, but I trust You to direct this way."

If God is redirecting you, He is not finished with you. He is leading you.

Reflection Questions:

1. Is there an area where God may be redirecting your steps?

2. Why can redirection feel like rejection at first?

____

____

3. How can you acknowledge God more fully in your plans and decisions?

____

____

Prayer:
Lord, I trust You to direct my path. Help me not to lean on my own understanding. If You are redirecting me, give me humility to follow and faith to believe that Your way is wise. Lead my steps and keep my heart surrendered to You. In Jesus' name, Amen.

Day 4: Trusting His Better Plan

Read: Jeremiah 29:11 "For I know the thoughts that I think toward you, saith the LORD, thoughts of peace, and not of evil…"

God's plan is not always easier, but it is always wiser.

Jeremiah 29:11 reminds us that God's thoughts toward His people are thoughts of peace and not of evil. This does not mean every season will be simple or painless. The original audience of this promise was walking through a difficult time. Yet God assured them that His purpose was still good.

Sometimes we call something good because it feels comfortable, quick, or familiar. But God's definition of good is deeper. His better plan may include growth, pruning, waiting, obedience, preparation, and trust.

Trusting His better plan means believing His heart when His hand moves differently than we expected.

It means we stop measuring God's goodness only by whether He gives us what we asked for. God's goodness is not limited to our preferred outcome. He may say yes, no, wait, or follow Me another way—and still be good in every answer.

A better plan is not always seen immediately. Joseph did not see the full purpose while he was in the pit or the prison. Ruth did not know the full story when she followed Naomi into a new land. Esther did not fully understand her position until courage was required. But God was working.

You may not understand every detail of your story right now, but you can trust the Author.

His plan is holy. His timing is wise. His love is faithful.

Reflection Questions:

1. Where do you need to trust that God's plan is better than your own?

2. Have you ever seen God bring good from a plan that looked disappointing at
    first?

3. How can you trust God's heart when His hand moves differently than
    expected?

Prayer:
Lord, I believe Your plan is wiser than mine. Help me trust Your heart when I do not
understand Your hand. Teach me to receive Your yes, no, wait, and redirection with
faith. I surrender my plan and trust Your better purpose. In Jesus' name, Amen.

Day 5: Following Where He Leads

Read: Psalm 32:8 "I will instruct thee and teach thee in the way which thou shalt go: I will guide thee with mine eye."

God does not only ask us to surrender our plans. He promises to guide us.

Psalm 32:8 is a beautiful promise of personal direction: "I will instruct thee and teach thee in the way which thou shalt go: I will guide thee with mine eye." The Lord is not distant from our decisions. He cares about the path we take.

Following where He leads requires trust, obedience, and attentiveness. We must be willing to move when He says move, wait when He says wait, stop when He says stop, and release when He says release.

Sometimes God leads through peace. Sometimes through correction. Sometimes through Scripture. Sometimes through wise counsel. Sometimes through a burden He places on the heart. Sometimes through doors that open or close. But His leading will never contradict His Word.

The surrendered heart does not demand its own way. It listens.

Following God may lead you beyond comfort, beyond familiarity, and beyond what others understand. But there is no safer place than the will of God. If He leads you, He will also keep you. If He calls you, He will equip you. If He redirects you, He will be with you on the new road.

You do not need to know every step before you follow the next one. You only need to know that the Shepherd is good.

A surrendered life says, "Lord, wherever You lead, help me follow."

Reflection Questions:

1. Where do you sense God leading you in this season?

2. What makes it difficult to follow when the next step feels uncertain?

3. How can you become more attentive to God's guidance?

Prayer:
Lord, instruct me and teach me in the way I should go. Guide me with Your eye. Help me follow where You lead, even when the path is unfamiliar. Give me a surrendered heart, listening ears, and obedient steps. In Jesus' name, Amen.

Week 9 Group Discussion Questions

1. What stood out to you most from this week's study?

2. Why is it difficult to surrender plans and dreams to God?

3. How can a good dream become unhealthy if it is not surrendered to the Lord?

4. What is the difference between redirection and rejection?

5. How can we make plans with wisdom while still keeping our hands open before God?

Week 9 Surrender Prayer

Lord, I surrender my plans and dreams to You. I give You my hopes, goals, expectations, timelines, and desires for the future. Lead what is from You, refine what needs to change, and help me release anything that is not Your will. When plans change, help me trust Your counsel. When You redirect me, help me follow with faith. I believe Your plan is wiser than mine, and I trust You to guide my steps. In Jesus' name, Amen.

Notes

Week 10: Surrendering Your Relationships

Loving Others with a Yielded Heart

Key Scripture:
"And be ye kind one to another, tenderhearted, forgiving one another…"
—Ephesians 4:32

Weekly Focus

This week is about surrendering relationships to the Lord. Family, friendships, marriage, church relationships, ministry relationships, and community can bring great joy, but they can also bring hurt, disappointment, expectations, and conflict. A surrendered heart learns to love others through God's wisdom, truth, forgiveness, and grace.

Opening Devotion

Relationships touch some of the deepest places of the heart.

God created us for love, fellowship, family, friendship, and community. We were not made to walk through life alone. The right relationships can encourage us, sharpen us, comfort us, pray for us, and help us grow closer to the Lord.

But relationships can also become places where surrender is deeply tested.

People may disappoint us. Loved ones may misunderstand us. Friends may change. Family may wound us. Ministry relationships may become difficult. Expectations may go unmet. Words may hurt. Trust may be broken. Offense may try to take root in the heart.

This is why our relationships must be surrendered to God.

Surrendering relationships does not mean we stop loving people. It means we stop trying to control them, carry them, fix them, or make them responsible for what only God can provide. It means we learn to love with open hands and a yielded heart.

The Lord teaches us to love with truth and grace. He teaches us to forgive without becoming foolish. He teaches us to serve without losing our peace. He teaches us to build healthy boundaries without bitterness. He teaches us to release people into His hands while obeying Him in how we treat them.

Ephesians 4:32 calls us to be kind, tenderhearted, and forgiving, even as God for Christ's sake has forgiven us. This kind of love is not natural to the flesh. It requires surrender. It requires the Holy Spirit working in the heart.

A surrendered relationship says, "Lord, teach me how to love this person in a way that honors You."

Sometimes God will ask us to forgive. Sometimes He will ask us to speak truth in love. Sometimes He will ask us to set wise boundaries. Sometimes He will ask us to release an unhealthy attachment. Sometimes He will ask us to stop carrying what belongs to Him.

This week, bring your relationships before the Lord. Bring the people you love, the people who hurt you, the people you worry about, and the people you struggle to forgive. God cares about every part of your heart.

A surrendered heart loves others best when it belongs fully to God first.

Day 1: Giving God the People You Love

Read: 1 Samuel 1:27–28 "For this child I prayed; and the LORD hath given me my petition which I asked of him: Therefore also I have lent him to the LORD…"

Hannah loved Samuel deeply. She had prayed for him with tears, and God answered her prayer. Yet when the child came, she gave him back to the Lord. Her love did not become possession. Her answered prayer became surrender.

The people we love are gifts from God, but they do not belong to us more than they belong to Him. Our children, spouses, family members, friends, and those we minister to are ultimately in God's hands.

This can be difficult because love often wants to protect, guide, rescue, and hold close. But sometimes our love becomes heavy with worry or control. We may carry burdens for people that God never asked us to carry. We may try to fix what only He can heal. We may try to direct what only He can lead.

Giving God the people we love means we pray faithfully, love sincerely, and trust Him deeply.

It means we say, "Lord, I love them, but You love them more. I cannot be their Savior. I cannot be their Holy Spirit. I cannot control their choices. I place them in Your hands."

This does not mean we become careless. It means we become prayerful and surrendered. We still love. We still serve. We still speak truth when needed. But we stop carrying the weight of being God in someone else's life.

The people you love are safest in the hands of the Lord.

Reflection Questions:

1. Who do you need to place more fully in God's hands?

2. Have you been carrying responsibility for someone that belongs to God?

3. How can you love faithfully without trying to control the outcome?

Prayer:
Lord, I give You the people I love. I place my family, friends, and relationships in Your faithful hands. Help me love them well without trying to control them. Teach me to pray, trust, and release them to Your care. In Jesus' name, Amen.

Day 2: Surrendering Hurt and Offense

Read: Proverbs 19:11 "The discretion of a man deferreth his anger; and it is his glory to pass over a transgression."

Hurt and offense can quietly take root in the heart.

Sometimes the offense comes from harsh words. Sometimes from being overlooked, misunderstood, betrayed, rejected, or treated unfairly. Sometimes it comes from unmet expectations. The pain may be real, but if it is not surrendered to God, it can begin to shape our thoughts, attitudes, and responses.

Offense often asks to be rehearsed. It wants us to replay what happened again and again. It wants us to build a case, defend ourselves inwardly, and hold the other person in debt. But surrender invites us to bring the hurt before the Lord and let Him deal with our hearts.

Surrendering hurt does not mean pretending nothing happened. It does not mean every situation is safe. It does not mean there are never consequences or boundaries. It means we refuse to let offense become the ruler of our heart.

Proverbs 19:11 says it is glory to pass over a transgression. This requires wisdom. Some matters can be released quietly with grace. Other matters require honest conversation, repentance, accountability, or distance. We need the Lord's discernment to know the difference.

The surrendered heart asks, "Lord, how do You want me to respond?"

Not every hurt needs to become bitterness. Not every offense needs to become a wall. Not every disappointment needs to become distance. God can heal, guide, and protect the heart.

Bring Him the hurt. Bring Him the words. Bring Him the memory. Let Him keep your heart tender and wise.

Reflection Questions:

1. Is there a hurt or offense you need to surrender to the Lord?

2.   Have you been rehearsing the offense more than bringing it to God?

____

____

3.   What would a wise, surrendered response look like?

____

____

Prayer:
Lord, I surrender my hurt and offense to You. Heal what has been wounded and give me wisdom in how to respond. Keep bitterness from taking root in my heart. Help me walk in truth, grace, and obedience. In Jesus' name, Amen.

Day 3: Loving Without Controlling

Read: 1 Corinthians 13:4–5

"Charity suffereth long, and is kind; charity envieth not; charity vaunteth not itself… seeketh not her own…"

God's love is not controlling.

True love is patient, kind, humble, and not self-seeking. It does not demand its own way. This is a powerful truth for relationships because sometimes what we call love can become mixed with control, fear, pressure, or unhealthy attachment.

We may try to control because we are afraid. Afraid someone will make a wrong choice. Afraid they will leave. Afraid they will be hurt. Afraid we will be hurt. Afraid life will not turn out the way we hoped.

But control does not produce peace. It produces pressure—for us and for others.

Loving without controlling means we honor God's place in another person's life. We can encourage, pray, teach, support, and speak truth in love, but we cannot force another person's heart. Only God can truly change a heart.

Jesus loved perfectly, yet He never manipulated people into following Him. He invited, taught, corrected, served, and spoke truth. But He did not control. His love was holy and free.

A surrendered heart learns to love with open hands.

Open-handed love says, "Lord, help me love this person according to Your will, not my fear."

It says, "Help me support without smothering, speak without controlling, care without carrying what belongs to You."

This kind of love is peaceful, wise, and surrendered.

Reflection Questions:

1. Is there a relationship where fear has made you want to control the outcome?

2. What is the difference between loving someone and trying to control someone?

3. How can you practice open-handed love this week?

Prayer:
Lord, teach me to love without controlling. Remove fear from my relationships and fill my heart with Your wisdom and peace. Help me encourage, pray, and speak truth in love while trusting You to work in the hearts of others. In Jesus' name, Amen.

Day 4: Boundaries with Grace and Wisdom

Read: Proverbs 4:23 "Keep thy heart with all diligence; for out of it are the issues of life."

Boundaries can be an expression of wisdom.

Some people think surrender means allowing others unlimited access to the heart, time, energy, or life. But Scripture tells us to guard the heart with all diligence. Guarding the heart does not mean becoming hard or unforgiving. It means living with wisdom before God.

Boundaries are not the opposite of love. Healthy boundaries can help love remain truthful, safe, and wise. They can protect peace, prevent bitterness, and make room for obedience to God.

Jesus Himself lived with boundaries. He withdrew to pray. He did not answer every demand placed on Him. He spoke truth even when others were offended. He loved people deeply, but He obeyed the Father above the expectations of people.

A surrendered heart does not confuse people-pleasing with godly love.

Sometimes a boundary may sound like:

"I cannot continue this conversation if it becomes dishonoring."
"I need time to pray before I answer."
"I love you, but I cannot take responsibility for your choices."
"I forgive you, but trust will need time and fruit to be rebuilt."
"I want peace, but I must also walk in wisdom."

Boundaries should not be used as punishment or revenge. They should be guided by prayer, Scripture, wisdom, and love. The goal is not to harden the heart, but to protect what God is healing and steward what He has entrusted to us.

Ask the Lord for wisdom. He knows when to draw near, when to speak, when to be silent, when to forgive quietly, and when to set a boundary with grace.

Reflection Questions:

1. Is there a relationship where you need wisdom for healthy boundaries?

2. Have you ever confused people-pleasing with love?

3. How can boundaries be practiced with grace instead of bitterness?

Prayer:
Lord, give me wisdom for healthy boundaries. Help me guard my heart without becoming hard. Teach me to love with grace, truth, and discernment. Free me from people-pleasing and help me obey You above every pressure. In Jesus' name, Amen.

Day 5: Forgiveness as Surrender

Read: Colossians 3:13 "Forbearing one another, and forgiving one another… even as Christ forgave you, so also do ye."

Forgiveness is surrender because it releases the debt into God's hands.

When someone hurts us, the heart may want to hold on until the person understands, apologizes, changes, or pays for what they did. But unforgiveness keeps the wound tied to the offender. It keeps the past active in the present and gives bitterness room to grow.

Forgiveness does not mean the hurt did not matter. It does not mean trust is automatically restored. It does not mean there are no consequences. It does not mean unsafe relationships become safe without repentance and wisdom.

Forgiveness means we choose to release vengeance, bitterness, and the right to make someone pay. We entrust justice, healing, and the outcome to God.

Christ forgave us with mercy we did not deserve. When we remember His grace toward us, we are strengthened to extend forgiveness to others. Not because the pain is small, but because God's mercy is great.

Sometimes forgiveness is a process. You may need to pray again and again, "Lord, help me forgive. Heal what still hurts. Remove bitterness from my heart." The Lord is patient with that process.

A surrendered heart forgives because it trusts God to be righteous and faithful.

Forgiveness opens the prison door—not only for the other person, but for your own heart. It allows the Lord to bring freedom where pain once lived.

Reflection Questions:

1. Is there someone you need God's grace to forgive?

2. What misunderstanding about forgiveness has made it difficult for you?

3. How can you surrender bitterness while still walking in wisdom?

Prayer:
Lord, help me forgive as Christ has forgiven me. I surrender bitterness, resentment, vengeance, and pain into Your hands. Heal what has been wounded and guide me with wisdom. Let forgiveness bring freedom to my heart. In Jesus' name, Amen.

Week 10 Group Discussion Questions

1. What stood out to you most from this week's study?

2. Why can relationships be one of the hardest areas to surrender?

3. What does it mean to give God the people we love?

4. How can we love others without trying to control them?

5. How can forgiveness and boundaries work together in a healthy, biblical way?

Week 10 Surrender Prayer

Lord, I surrender my relationships to You. I give You the people I love, the people who have hurt me, the people I worry about, and the people I struggle to understand. Teach me to love with truth, grace, humility, and wisdom. Help me forgive as Christ has forgiven me. Show me where healthy boundaries are needed and keep my heart free from bitterness. I trust You with every relationship in my life. In Jesus' name, Amen.

Notes

Week 11: Surrendering Your Calling and Service

Serving God with Humility and Obedience

Key Scripture:
"And whatsoever ye do, do it heartily, as to the Lord, and not unto men."
—Colossians 3:23

Weekly Focus

This week is about surrendering calling, service, ministry, gifts, purpose, recognition, and obedience to the Lord. God gives each of His children gifts and assignments, but those gifts must be offered back to Him with humility, faithfulness, and a heart that desires His glory above all.

Opening Devotion

Serving the Lord is a beautiful privilege.

God does not call us because we are perfect. He calls us because He is gracious. He takes ordinary lives, surrendered hearts, willing hands, and obedient steps, and He uses them for His purpose.

But even service must be surrendered.

Sometimes we can begin serving God with pure desire, but over time the heart can become tired, pressured, discouraged, or distracted. We may begin to compare our calling with someone else's. We may serve for approval instead of obedience. We may become weary from striving. We may feel overlooked when no one notices. We may carry ministry burdens that belong to God alone.

Colossians 3:23 reminds us, "And whatsoever ye do, do it heartily, as to the Lord, and not unto men." This verse helps purify the motive of service. Whatever God has given us to do, we are to do it for Him.

Not for applause.
Not for praise.
Not for position.
Not for comparison.
Not for the approval of people.

For the Lord.

Surrendering your calling means placing your gifts, assignments, influence, opportunities, and labor at the feet of Jesus. It means saying, "Lord, this belongs to You. Use it how You desire. Open the doors You want opened. Close what is not Your will. Keep my heart humble. Let my service bring glory to Your name."

A surrendered servant does not need to be seen by everyone, because she knows she is seen by God.

A surrendered servant does not have to strive for worth, because her worth is already found in Christ.

A surrendered servant does not measure faithfulness by fame, numbers, or recognition, but by obedience to the Lord.

This week, bring your calling and service before God. Whether you serve in your home, church, workplace, community, ministry, writing, teaching, counseling, caring, praying, giving, or encouraging others, the Lord sees it all.

Nothing done for Him is wasted.

A surrendered calling says, "Lord, use me for Your glory, and keep my heart close to You."

Day 1: Called for God's Glory

Read: 1 Peter 4:10–11 "As every man hath received the gift, even so minister the same one to another… that God in all things may be glorified through Jesus Christ…"

Every gift is meant to glorify God.

The gifts God gives are not for pride, comparison, or self-promotion. They are entrusted to us so we can serve others and point people back to Him. Whether the gift seems public or hidden, large or small, visible or quiet, it matters when it is used for God's glory.

Sometimes people think calling only means standing on a platform or doing something widely recognized. But many sacred callings happen in quiet places. A mother teaching her children to pray. A woman encouraging a hurting friend. A servant cleaning the church when no one sees. A counselor listening with compassion. A writer putting truth on the page. A prayer warrior interceding in secret.

God sees every act of obedience.

Surrendering your calling begins with remembering who the calling is for. It is not first about our name, success, approval, or comfort. It is about the Lord being glorified through our lives.

When the heart desires God's glory above all, service becomes worship. We begin to pray, "Lord, let them see You, not me. Let my life point to Christ. Let my gifts be used in a way that honors You."

You do not have to imitate someone else's assignment. God knows what He placed in you. Be faithful with what He has entrusted to your hands.

Reflection Questions:

1. What gifts or opportunities has God entrusted to you?

2. How can those gifts be used to glorify God and serve others?

____

____

3. Is there any area where comparison has distracted you from your own calling?

____

____

Prayer:
Lord, thank You for the gifts and calling You have placed in my life. Help me use them for Your glory and not for my own praise. Keep me from comparison and teach me to serve faithfully where You have assigned me. In Jesus' name, Amen.

Day 2: Serving Without Striving

Read: Matthew 11:28–30

"Come unto me, all ye that labour and are heavy laden, and I will give you rest."

It is possible to serve God and still become weary from striving.

Striving often happens when we begin carrying more than God asked us to carry. We try to prove ourselves, please everyone, fix everything, meet every need, and make every outcome happen. The work may be good, but the weight becomes too heavy because we are carrying it in our own strength.

Jesus invites the weary to come to Him. This includes weary servants.

Serving without striving means we work from surrender, not pressure. We obey God, but we do not try to be God. We serve people, but we do not become their Savior. We steward the assignment, but we trust the results to the Lord.

There is a difference between faithfulness and frantic labor.

Faithfulness is peaceful obedience. Striving is anxious performance. Faithfulness depends on God's strength. Striving depends on self-effort. Faithfulness says, "Lord, I will obey You." Striving says, "Everything depends on me."

The Lord does not call you to burn out trying to prove your love for Him. He calls you to abide in Him and bear fruit from that place of closeness.

If service has become heavy, bring that burden to Jesus. Ask Him what He assigned to you and what you have picked up out of fear, pressure, or people-pleasing.

His yoke is easy, and His burden is light.

Reflection Questions:

1. Where have you been serving from pressure instead of peace?

2. Are you carrying any burden in ministry or service that God did not ask you to carry?

____

____

3. What would serving from rest and surrender look like for you?

____

____

Prayer:
Lord, I surrender striving to You. Help me serve from rest, not pressure. Teach me the difference between faithfulness and trying to carry what belongs to You. Let my service flow from closeness with Christ. In Jesus' name, Amen.

Day 3: Surrendering Recognition

Read: Matthew 6:4 "That thine alms may be in secret: and thy Father which seeth in secret himself shall reward thee openly."

God sees what people may never notice.

There are many acts of service done in hidden places. Prayers no one hears. Tears no one sees. Sacrifices no one thanks you for. Faithfulness that receives no applause. Love poured out quietly. Work done behind the scenes.

The flesh may want recognition. It may want someone to notice, affirm, praise, or validate the sacrifice. Encouragement is not wrong. Appreciation is a blessing. But when recognition becomes the reason we serve, the heart becomes vulnerable to disappointment, pride, and offense.

Surrendering recognition means we allow God to be the One who sees, measures, and rewards our service.

Jesus teaches that the Father sees in secret. This is deeply comforting. Nothing done for God is invisible to Him. The prayer whispered in the quiet room matters. The meal prepared with love matters. The lesson taught faithfully matters. The encouragement sent at the right time matters. The ministry done without applause matters.

If God sees it, it is not wasted.

A surrendered servant can serve quietly because she is secure in the Father's sight. She does not need to announce every sacrifice. She does not need to compete for attention. She does not need praise to know her obedience matters.

The Lord sees. That is enough.

Reflection Questions:

1. Have you ever felt unseen or unappreciated in your service?

2. How does it comfort you to know the Father sees in secret?

____

____

3. Is there any recognition or approval you need to surrender to God?

____

____

Prayer:
Lord, I surrender my desire for recognition to You. Thank You for seeing what others may never notice. Purify my motives and help me serve for Your glory alone. Let Your approval be enough for my heart. In Jesus' name, Amen.

Day 4: Faithful in Small Things

Read: Luke 16:10

"He that is faithful in that which is least is faithful also in much..."

Small things matter to God.

The world often celebrates large platforms, visible success, big numbers, and public recognition. But the kingdom of God values faithfulness. The Lord sees the small acts of obedience that may never be applauded on earth but are precious in heaven.

Being faithful in small things may look like praying daily, keeping your word, serving one person, writing one page, encouraging one soul, forgiving one offense, showing up when no one sees, or doing the right thing when it feels unnoticed.

Small obedience builds a surrendered life.

Many people want large assignments, but God often forms us through hidden faithfulness first. David was faithful in the field before he stood before a giant. Joseph was faithful in prison before he stood in the palace. Ruth was faithful in the field before her story became part of God's redemptive plan.

Do not despise the small assignment.

What feels small to you may be deeply significant in God's plan. A small act of obedience today may become a seed for future fruit. A quiet yes may prepare the heart for a greater yes later.

A surrendered servant does not demand a larger assignment before being faithful with the present one. She says, "Lord, whatever You place in my hands today, help me do it for You."

Faithfulness in small things is worship.

Reflection Questions:

1. What small assignment has God placed in your hands right now?

2. Have you ever been tempted to overlook small acts of obedience?

3. How can you be faithful today with what God has already given you?

Prayer:
Lord, help me be faithful in small things. Teach me not to despise quiet obedience or hidden assignments. Let me serve You with joy in what is before me today. Use every small yes for Your glory. In Jesus' name, Amen.

Day 5: Saying Yes to God's Assignment

Read: Isaiah 6:8 "Also I heard the voice of the Lord, saying, Whom shall I send, and who will go for us? Then said I, Here am I; send me."

A surrendered servant says yes to God.

Isaiah's response to the Lord was simple and powerful: "Here am I; send me." He did not have every detail. He did not know everything the assignment would require. But his heart was available.

God is still looking for willing hearts.

Saying yes to God's assignment does not mean you feel completely ready. It does not mean you have no fear. It does not mean you know every step. It means you trust the One who calls you.

Many times, we hesitate because we feel unqualified, afraid, too broken, too old, too young, too busy, too unseen, or too ordinary. But God does not depend on our perfection. He works through surrendered availability.

If God calls you, He will equip you. If He sends you, He will go with you. If He assigns the work, He will provide grace for the work.

Your yes may be public or private. It may be a yes to teach, write, pray, serve, forgive, encourage, lead, give, care, or obey in a hidden place. Whatever the assignment, the Lord desires a willing heart.

A surrendered calling does not say, "Lord, use me only if it is easy." It says, "Lord, I belong to You. Lead me, and help me obey."

Reflection Questions:

1. What assignment or step of obedience might God be asking you to say yes to?

2. What fear or insecurity makes it difficult to say yes?

3. How does knowing God equips those He calls encourage you?

Prayer:
Lord, here I am. I surrender my calling and service to You. Help me say yes to Your assignment with faith and humility. Equip me for what You have called me to do, and keep my heart close to You as I serve. In Jesus' name, Amen.

Week 11 Group Discussion Questions

1. What stood out to you most from this week's study?

2. Why is it important to surrender our gifts and calling back to God?

3. What is the difference between serving faithfully and striving anxiously?

4. How does knowing God sees in secret help us serve with pure motives?

5. What small act of obedience may God be asking you to be faithful in right now?

Week 11 Surrender Prayer

Lord, I surrender my calling and service to You. I give You my gifts, assignments, opportunities, ministry, labor, and desire to be used for Your glory. Keep my heart humble and pure. Help me serve without striving, obey without seeking applause, and remain faithful in small things. When You call, help me say yes with courage and trust. Use my life for Your purpose, and let all I do point back to You. In Jesus' name, Amen.

Notes

Week 12: Living Fully Surrendered

A Daily Life of Worship, Trust, and Obedience

Key Scripture:
"I am crucified with Christ: nevertheless I live; yet not I, but Christ liveth in me…"
—Galatians 2:20

Weekly Focus

This final week is about living fully surrendered to the Lord every day. Surrender is not only a moment at the altar or a prayer during a difficult season. It is a daily way of walking with Jesus—trusting Him, obeying Him, worshiping Him, and allowing His life to be seen through ours.

Opening Devotion

Surrender is not only something we do once. It is a life we learn to live.

Over these twelve weeks, we have brought many parts of life before the Lord: the heart, the mind, the will, the past, the future, fear, worry, waiting, plans, dreams, relationships, calling, and service. Each area matters to God because He desires all of us, not only the parts we find easy to give.

A fully surrendered life is not a perfect life. It is a yielded life.

It is the life that keeps returning to the Lord and saying, "Here I am again, Father. Shape me. Lead me. Cleanse me. Use me. Help me trust You more."

Galatians 2:20 gives us a beautiful picture of surrender: "I am crucified with Christ: nevertheless I live; yet not I, but Christ liveth in me." The surrendered life is not about trying harder in our own strength. It is about Christ living in us.

This means our old way of ruling ourselves must bow before His lordship. Our pride, fear, control, selfish ambition, bitterness, and self-dependence must be brought to the cross. In their place, Christ forms humility, faith, love, obedience, peace, and worship.

Living fully surrendered means Jesus becomes Lord over every room of the heart.

Not just Sunday.
Not just ministry.
Not just public life.
Not just the parts others can see.

All of it.

Our words.
Our thoughts.
Our motives.
Our decisions.
Our relationships.
Our dreams.
Our wounds.
Our time.
Our gifts.
Our future.

A surrendered life says, "Lord, all of me belongs to all of You."

There will still be moments when surrender feels hard. There will still be days when fear rises, control returns, or the heart feels weak. But surrender is practiced by returning. Again and again, we come back to Jesus. Again and again, we lay down what we picked up. Again and again, we trust His hands.

This final week is not an ending. It is an invitation to continue walking with the Lord in daily surrender.

A surrendered heart is not empty—it is held by God.

Day 1: Surrender as a Daily Decision

Read: Luke 9:23 "And he said to them all, If any man will come after me, let him deny himself, and take up his cross daily, and follow me."

Jesus said that following Him involves taking up the cross daily. This means surrender is not only a one-time decision. It is a daily choice to deny self, follow Christ, and trust His way above our own.

Every day brings opportunities to surrender.

We surrender when we choose prayer instead of panic.
We surrender when we obey instead of resist.
We surrender when we forgive instead of holding bitterness.
We surrender when we trust instead of control.
We surrender when we speak truth instead of fear.
We surrender when we follow Jesus even when the flesh wants another way.

Daily surrender does not mean every day will feel deeply emotional or dramatic. Many times, surrender looks quiet and simple. It may look like beginning the morning with prayer. It may look like choosing patience in a difficult conversation. It may look like releasing worry before going to sleep. It may look like saying, "Lord, help me honor You today."

The surrendered life is built through daily yielded choices.

Some days you may feel strong. Other days you may feel weak. But the strength of surrender is not found in your ability to be perfect. It is found in the faithfulness of Christ, who helps you follow Him one day at a time.

Today is an opportunity to surrender again.

Reflection Questions:

1. What does daily surrender look like in your current season?

2.   What is one area you tend to pick back up after giving it to God?

____

____

3.   What daily habit can help you keep your heart surrendered to the Lord?

____

____

Prayer:
Lord, help me surrender daily. Teach me to take up my cross and follow You with a willing heart. When I am tempted to take control again, gently lead me back to trust. Let my daily choices honor You. In Jesus' name, Amen.

Day 2: Christ Living in Me

Read: Galatians 2:20 "I am crucified with Christ: nevertheless I live; yet not I, but Christ liveth in me…"

The surrendered life is not simply self-improvement. It is Christ living in us.

Many people try to change in their own strength. They try to be more patient, more faithful, more loving, more peaceful, more disciplined, and more obedient by willpower alone. But true transformation comes through the life of Christ working within us.

Paul said, "Yet not I, but Christ liveth in me." This is the secret of surrendered living. It is no longer the old self ruling the heart. It is Christ dwelling, leading, strengthening, and shaping the life from within.

When Christ lives in us, our desires begin to change. Our motives begin to be purified. Our reactions begin to be softened. Our obedience begins to deepen. Our love begins to reflect His love.

This does not happen because we are strong enough. It happens because He is faithful enough.

Surrender means we stop trying to live the Christian life apart from Christ. We abide in Him. We depend on Him. We ask Him to live through us.

Before you respond, ask: "Jesus, live through me."
Before you serve, ask: "Jesus, love through me."
Before you decide, ask: "Jesus, lead me."
Before you speak, ask: "Jesus, guard my words."
Before you face the day, ask: "Jesus, be glorified in me."

The surrendered life is the life of Christ expressed through a yielded vessel.

Reflection Questions:

1. What does "Christ liveth in me" mean to you personally?

2. Where have you been trying to change or serve in your own strength?

____

____

3. How can you depend on Christ more deeply in your daily life?

____

____

Prayer:
Lord Jesus, live through me. I surrender my self-effort and ask You to work in me by Your grace. Shape my heart, guide my words, purify my motives, and let Your life be seen through mine. In Jesus' name, Amen.

Day 3: Walking in Obedience

Read: John 14:15 "If ye love me, keep my commandments."

Obedience is one of the clearest fruits of surrender.

Jesus said, "If ye love me, keep my commandments." Love for Christ is not only spoken with words. It is revealed through obedience. A surrendered heart desires to please the Lord, even when obedience is costly, uncomfortable, or unseen.

Obedience is not legalism when it flows from love. It is worship.

We do not obey to earn God's love. We obey because we have received His love. We do not obey to prove we are worthy. We obey because Jesus is worthy. We do not obey because every command is easy. We obey because the Lord is faithful and His ways are right.

Walking in obedience means we ask God to lead every part of life. We do not separate our spiritual life from our daily choices. The surrendered heart asks:

Lord, how do You want me to speak?
Lord, how do You want me to forgive?
Lord, how do You want me to serve?
Lord, how do You want me to use my time?
Lord, how do You want me to honor You in this decision?

Sometimes obedience will be joyful. Sometimes obedience will require sacrifice. But every act of obedience matters to God.

The surrendered life walks with a listening heart and willing feet.

Reflection Questions:

1. How does obedience show love for Jesus?

2. Is there an area where God has been asking you to obey more fully?

3. What makes obedience difficult, and how can surrender help?

Prayer:
Lord, teach me to walk in obedience. Let my love for You be shown not only in words, but in the way I live. Give me a willing heart, listening ears, and faithful steps. Help me obey You with joy and trust. In Jesus' name, Amen.

Day 4: Peace in Full Surrender

Read: Isaiah 26:3 "Thou wilt keep him in perfect peace, whose mind is stayed on thee: because he trusteth in thee."

There is peace in full surrender.

This does not mean life becomes free from problems. It means the heart is no longer fighting God for control. A surrendered heart can rest because it trusts the Lord's wisdom, timing, love, and faithfulness.

Control produces pressure. Surrender produces peace.

When we try to hold everything together in our own strength, we become weary. We carry burdens that belong to God. We worry over outcomes we cannot control. We exhaust ourselves trying to protect, fix, predict, and manage every part of life.

But when we surrender, we place the weight where it belongs—in God's hands.

Isaiah 26:3 promises perfect peace to the one whose mind is stayed on the Lord. Peace comes as our focus returns to Him. Not to the storm. Not to the unanswered question. Not to the fear. Not to the pressure. To Him.

A fully surrendered life does not say, "Everything is easy." It says, "God is faithful."

It does not say, "I understand everything." It says, "I trust Him."

It does not say, "I am in control." It says, "The Lord is my keeper."

Peace is one of the beautiful fruits of a yielded heart. The more we surrender to God, the less we are ruled by fear, striving, and anxiety.

The Lord can keep you in peace as you trust Him.

Reflection Questions:

1. Where do you need the peace that comes from surrender?

2. How has trying to control everything affected your peace?

3. What would it look like to keep your mind stayed on the Lord today?

Prayer:
Lord, I surrender the need to control everything. Keep my mind stayed on You and fill my heart with Your peace. Help me trust Your wisdom, timing, and faithful care. Teach me to rest in full surrender. In Jesus' name, Amen.

Day 5: All of Me for All of Him

Read: Romans 12:1 "I beseech you therefore, brethren, by the mercies of God, that ye present your bodies a living sacrifice…"

All of me for all of Him.

This is the heart of surrender. Not a little portion of the life. Not only the comfortable parts. Not only the public parts. Not only the parts we already understand. All of me belongs to all of Him.

Romans 12:1 calls us to present ourselves as living sacrifices unto God. A living sacrifice is not placed before God once and then forgotten. It is a daily offering. A continual yielding. A life that says, "Lord, I am Yours."

All of me means my heart.
All of me means my mind.
All of me means my will.
All of me means my past.
All of me means my future.
All of me means my fears.
All of me means my dreams.
All of me means my relationships.
All of me means my calling.
All of me means my whole life.

For all of Him means Jesus is worthy of everything.

He is worthy of our trust.
He is worthy of our obedience.
He is worthy of our worship.
He is worthy of our surrender.
He is worthy of the hidden yes and the public yes.
He is worthy in the waiting and in the answered prayer.
He is worthy in the valley and on the mountain.

Surrender is not losing ourselves to emptiness. It is giving ourselves to the One who loves us, saves us, keeps us, and leads us.

A surrendered heart is not empty—it is held by God.

As this study closes, let this become more than a title. Let it become a prayer:

Lord, all of me for all of You.

Reflection Questions:

1. Looking back over this study, what area of surrender has been most meaningful to you?

2. What area will you continue surrendering to the Lord after this study ends?

3. What does "All of Me for All of Him" mean in your life today?

Prayer:
Lord, all of me belongs to all of You. I present my life to You as a living sacrifice. Take my heart, mind, will, past, future, fears, dreams, relationships, calling, and every step ahead. Let my surrender become worship. Let my life bring glory to Your name. In Jesus' name, Amen.

Week 12 Group Discussion Questions

1. What stood out to you most from this final week's study?

2. How has your understanding of surrender grown through this Bible study?

3. Why is surrender a daily decision and not only a one-time moment?

4. What does it mean to live with Christ living in you?

5. What is one practical way you will continue living "All of Me for All of Him"?

Week 12 Surrender Prayer

Lord, thank You for walking with me through this journey of surrender. I give You my whole life again. Let my heart remain soft, my mind renewed, my will yielded, my past healed, my future trusted to You, my fears cast upon You, my dreams placed in Your hands, my relationships guided by Your wisdom, and my calling used for Your glory. Teach me to live each day with a surrendered heart. All of me belongs to all of You. In Jesus' name, Amen.

Final Reflection: My Surrender Commitment

Use this space to write a personal prayer of surrender to the Lord. Tell Him what you are giving to Him, what you are trusting Him with, and how you desire to live for Him moving forward.

Notes

Closing Prayer

Lord, thank You for walking with me through this journey of surrender. Thank You for being patient with my heart and faithful in every season. I give You my whole life—my heart, my mind, my will, my past, my future, my fears, my dreams, my relationships, my calling, and every step ahead.

Teach me to live daily with open hands and a yielded heart. When I am tempted to take back control, remind me that Your hands are faithful. When I am afraid, remind me that Your love is perfect. When I do not understand, remind me that Your wisdom is greater than mine.

Lord, all of me belongs to all of You.

Use my life for Your glory. Shape my heart for Your purpose. Lead me in Your will. Let my surrender become worship before You.

In Jesus' name, Amen.

About the Author

Dr. Lende Click is a Christian author, speaker, counselor, and founder of Lende Click Publishing. She writes faith-filled books that encourage women, children, and families to grow in courage, healing, identity, and trust in God.

Born and raised in Cebu, Philippines, Dr. Click's life has been marked by trials, grace, healing, and redemption. Through many fires, she has seen the faithfulness of God again and again. Her testimony and ministry are rooted in the belief that the Lord brings beauty from ashes, strength from suffering, and purpose from pain.

Through her writing, Dr. Click seeks to encourage hearts, strengthen faith, and remind readers that God is present even in life's hardest seasons. She is the author of several inspirational Christian books, Bible studies, devotionals, children's books, and faith-based stories, including works from the Faith & Courage collection and books for women seeking spiritual growth, healing, and restoration.

In addition to writing, Dr. Click serves as a Christian counselor. She is an NCCA Licensed Professional Clinical Counselor, Certified Temperament Counselor, NCCA Licensed Clinical Pastoral Counselor, and NCCA Licensed Christian Counselor. She is also advanced certified in Death and Grief Therapy and Integrated Marriage and Family Therapy, and she is a member of the American Association of Christian Counselors (AACC) and the National Christian Counselors Association (NCCA).

Dr. Click writes with a special heart for women who are hurting, children in need, and those who long to know God more deeply. Through her books and ministry, she desires to point every reader to Jesus Christ—the One who saves, restores, carries, and never leaves His children alone in the fire.

Some proceeds from her work help support children in Cebu, Philippines. She currently lives in Augusta, Georgia, and continues to write books that inspire faith, courage, healing, and hope.

Other Books by Dr. Lende Click

The Gift of Godly Friendship
A Bible study for women who long for meaningful, godly connection.

Daughters of the King
An 8-week Bible study workbook for women growing in faith, identity, and purpose.

Prayers of a Daughter of the King
A devotional journey of prayer, strength, and deeper intimacy with God.

God Is Still Writing Your Story
A faith-filled message of hope for those learning to trust God in unfinished seasons.

When God Carries a Woman Through the Fire
A powerful encouragement for women walking through pain, testing, and restoration.

A Life Redeemed
A story of God's grace, healing, and redeeming love.

Serving the Lord with a Willing Heart
A 12-Week Bible Study on Faithful Service for the Lord

Healing for the Woman Who Has Been Hurt
A Bible Study for Finding Hope, Restoration, and Wholeness in Christ

Faith & Courage Children's Books

Sammy the Shy Snail's Big Race
A gentle story of courage, faith, and believing God can help you do hard things.

Bella the Brave Butterfly and the Stormy Day
A sweet story teaching children courage and trust in God during fearful times.

Toby the Turtle Who Trusted God
A faith-filled story about learning to trust God one step at a time.

Lende's Story: Faith Like Sunshine
An uplifting story of faith, hope, and God's light shining through every season.

Christian Fantasy

The Kingdom of Everlight
An epic faith-filled fantasy story of courage, destiny, and the triumph of light over darkness.
Book One in The Kingdom of Everlight Series

The Kingdom of Everlight: The Crown of Hidden Fire
An Epic Christian Fantasy of Courage, Sacrifice, and the Light That Darkness Cannot Destroy
Book Two in The Kingdom of Everlight Series

The Kingdom of Everlight: The Crown of Everlight – COMING SOON
An Epic Christian Fantasy of Restoration, Courage, and the Light That Darkness Could Not Overcome
Book Three in The Kingdom of Everlight Series

Christian Historical Romance Novel

The Light Beneath the Crown
A Christian Novel of Faith, Love, and Redemption